The
Source®
for
Learning Disabilities

Paula S. Currie

Elizabeth M. Wadlington

Skill Area:	Learning Disabilities
Ages:	3 - adult
Grades:	PreK - adult

LinguiSystems, Inc.
3100 4th Avenue
East Moline, IL 61244-9700

1-800 PRO IDEA
1-800-776-4332

Fax: 1-800-577-4555
E-Mail: service@linguisystems.com
Web: www.linguisystems.com
TDD: 1-800-933-8331
          (for those with hearing impairments)

Printed in the U.S.A.
ISBN 0-7606-0327-8

About the Authors

Paula S. Currie, Ph.D., is an Associate Professor and Interim Head in the Department of Communication Sciences & Disorders at Southeastern Louisiana University (SLU) in Hammond, LA. Dr. Currie is also the Program Director for the undergraduate and graduate programs in speech-language pathology at SLU. She teaches courses in assessment and treatment of communication and learning disorders, and has developed and teaches a course about language and literacy. Dr. Currie has extensive experience diagnosing and treating individuals with communication disorders. She has worked in public school, private practice, hospital, and university settings. She serves as a consultant to Louisiana's Assistive Technical Network. She lives in Ponchatoula, LA, with her husband, Mark, and her two sons, Taylor and Zachary. This is her third book with LinguiSystems. She also co-authored *125 Ways to Be a Better Reader* with Elizabeth Wadlington.

Elizabeth M. Wadlington, Ph.D., is a Professor in the Department of Teaching and Learning at Southeastern Louisiana University (SLU) in Hammond, LA. Her responsibilities include graduate and undergraduate courses in reading, elementary education, and early childhood education. She has a special interest in learning difficulties because her own son has struggled and coped successfully with dyslexia. As a result, she is actively involved in consultation, assessment, and teaching those with reading problems. She has also served on numerous committees and boards to develop and implement learning and teaching improvements. In addition, she has had many journal articles published and has presented at national/international conferences. Prior to coming to SLU, Elizabeth taught kindergarten and elementary school, trained and assessed Head Start teachers, and worked in adult literacy. She currently lives in Mandeville, LA, with her husband, Charles. *The Source for Learning Disabilities* is her second book with LinguiSystems. She also co-authored *125 Ways to Be a Better Reader* with Paula Currie.

Dedications

Paula: to all of the people with learning disabilities and to the special education colleagues with whom I have worked

Beth: with love and gratitude to Patrick, Charles, and Sandra

Table of Contents

Whave professional and personal reasons for writing *The Source for Learning Disabilities*. On the professional side, we wrote it so teachers, parents, and people with learning disabilities can benefit from our experiences. You'll find a lot of information in *The Source for Learning Disabilities*—screening checklists, characteristics, resources (including many Internet sites), and most importantly, intervention strategies. Read our personal reasons for writing the book.

Paula

I learned the hard way that the best way to treat children with LD is with teamwork. Way back when, the role of the speech-language pathologist was to work only with children identified with speech impairments; special education teachers worked with students with learning disabilities. But I knew from working with children that many with learning disabilities also had speech and language disorders such as auditory memory and sequencing deficits, limited receptive and expressive vocabularies, and a dislike of writing. I was so frustrated! I knew I could help these children, and I knew an integrated teaching approach was better than "pull-out" therapy.

So, I became a certified teacher of learning disabilities and was finally able to work with children with LD. My most difficult problem wasn't working with the children, but with the special education teachers and other professionals who questioned the role of SLPs in learning disabilities. "What do you know about reading and spelling?" they asked. "I know language, and these children have language disorders that affect their ability to succeed academically and socially," I would respond. Sadly, after all of these years, I still have to answer these questions. Whose job is it to work with people who have learning disabilities? A team of qualified professionals, concerned parents and family, and the person with the disability.

Beth

I was a kindergarten and elementary teacher, and I had some very bright children that just couldn't seem to learn reading, writing, or math. I had other students who couldn't pay attention or sit still no matter what I did or how hard they tried. These pupils puzzled me, and it became my professional mission to find ways to help them.

Then learning problems hit closer to home. My son, Patrick, was intelligent, creative, and made good grades in school, yet it took him much more time and effort than other students to do schoolwork. He found strategies that helped, but matters grew worse as he got older. In high school, he was placed in honors classes that his dad and I begged him to drop because of the physical and psychological toll they took on him. Patrick was a freshman in college before he was diagnosed with dyslexia and dysgraphia. His coping skills, super-human efforts, and good grades had hidden the truth from everyone! Finally being able to label his learning difficulties was a relief: he was able to accept, talk about, and deal with his learning differences. Patrick is now a student in a Ph.D. program.

Here is how *The Source for Learning Disabilities* is organized.

Chapter 1—Overview

We'll talk about general definitions, prevalence numbers, and etiology of LD.

Chapter 2—Social and Emotional Aspects of LD

Chapters 2 and 8 are bookend chapters: they discuss issues that apply to Chapters 3-7.

Chapters 3-7—Communication Disorders, Dyslexia, Dysgraphia, Dyscalculia, and Attention Deficit Disorder (ADD)

Chapters 3-7 form the heart of the book. They are divided into the following sections:

- ✔ Scenario
- ✔ Definition
- ✔ Characteristics (and Characteristics Chart)
- ✔ Screening (and Screening Checklist)
- ✔ Intervention
- ✔ Intervention Strategies
- ✔ Summary
- ✔ References and Resources

Chapter 8—Management and Intervention Issues

This bookend chapter discusses detailed ways of devising management and intervention strategies for learning disabilities.

Glossary

We hope the descriptions, checklists, and interventions in *The Source for Learning Disabilities* will help you, as clinicians and teachers, to work more effectively with people with LD and their families. We also hope children and adults with learning disabilities realize they have tremendous strengths, and can be successful in school and in life.

Paula and Beth

Overview

Stacy went to her professor's office one afternoon to discuss a quiz that had been returned. She told the professor, "I don't know why I did so poorly on the quiz. I studied and knew the material. I thought I answered all of the questions, but now that we have gone over the quiz in class, I see I didn't write enough. I've always had trouble with essay questions. What can I do to improve my essay writing?"

The professor responded, "Let's look at one of the questions and your answer. This question asks you to justify your answer. Your answer has to be organized, and it must contain a sufficient amount of accurate information in order to receive full credit. General statements without facts to support your position aren't sufficient." The professor had Stacy outline her answers before writing them. An outline helped her organize the information, and she could practice writing answers to sample questions. She and her study partner could practice verbally answering sample test questions. Together they could learn the course content and work on improving the organization of their answers.

Educators recognize students like Stacy. These students are verbally articulate, can demonstrate their knowledge on activity-based assignments, but struggle with written assignments. Their written work is characterized by poor organization, lack of clarity, and errors in syntax, spelling, and punctuation. These students have learning disabilities.

This chapter is an overview of learning disabilities (LD). You will learn some of the commonly accepted medical and educational definitions, prevalence figures, and possible etiological explanations for various disorders. We will also discuss and identify common characteristics associated with learning disabilities and take a quick look at the disorders discussed in *The Source for Learning Disabilities*.

Definitions . . . .

Professionals continue to struggle to define learning disabilities. Some definitions specify problems in certain abilities, domains, or skills (e.g., reading, attention, processing, adaptive behavior); others include discrepancy as a distinctive feature (e.g., aptitude vs. performance, performance and age or grade-level expectations); and some identify learning disabilities by exclusion (e.g., not due to mental retardation, not a cultural difference, not a sensory deficit, nor a behavioral condition). Most definitions are classified under a medical or educational model.

The Diagnostic and Statistical Manual of Mental Disorders (DSM-IV)

The DSM-IV classifies learning disabilities under the heading: *Learning Disorders.* Information about the disorders in the DSM-IV are titled: *Disorders Usually First Diagnosed in Infancy, Childhood, or Adolescence.* Learning disorders include the categories: *Reading Disorders, Mathematics Disorders, Disorder of Written Expression*, and *Learning Disorder Not Otherwise Specified.*

DSM-IV ——————————————————————————— Definition **1**

"Learning disorders are diagnosed when the individual's achievement on individually administered, standardized tests in reading, mathematics, or written expression is substantially below that expected for age, schooling, and level of intelligence. The learning problems significantly interfere with academic achievement or activities of daily living that require reading, mathematical, or writing skills."

DSM-IV defines "substantially below" as a discrepancy of more than two standard deviations between achievement and intelligence. Smaller discrepancies can be used in cases where a person's performance on the academic or intelligence test is compromised by associated disorders (e.g., cognitive processing and health conditions). If a vision and hearing problem coexists, the learning difficulties must be greater than those usually associated with the sensory problem. The category, *Learning Disorder Not Otherwise Specified*, includes disorders in reading, mathematics, and written expression that interfere with academic achievement and daily living activities. The person's performance on appropriate standardized tests is not significantly below age, grade-level expectations, or measures of intelligence. The category applies when the criteria for any of the other learning disorders categories are not met. This definition characterizes LD under the medical model.

The National Institute of Mental Health (NIMH)

The NIMH is the federal agency that supports research of the brain, mental illnesses, and mental health. It defines learning disabilities more broadly than the DSM-IV, including difficulties with processing information, speaking, reading and writing, motor skills, and behavior. This definition of LD is also under a medical model.

NIMH ————————————————————————— Definition **2**

"Learning Disabilities (LD) is a disorder that affects people's ability to either interpret what they see and hear or to link information from different parts of the brain. These limitations can show up in many ways—as specific difficulties with spoken and written language, coordination, self-control, or attention. Such difficulties extend to school-work and can impede learning to read or write, or to do math" (National Center for Learning Disabilities 1997).

The National Joint Committee on Learning Disabilities (NJCLD)

The definition of learning disabilities developed by the NJCLD is commonly used by educators and can be found in legislation that regulates institutions and companies who serve individuals with disabilities. This definition of LD is under an education model.

NJCLD ———————————————————————— Definition **3**

"Learning disabilities is a generic term that refers to a heterogeneous group of disorders manifested by significant difficulties in the acquisition and use of listening, speaking, reading, writing, reasoning, or mathematical abilities. These disorders are intrinsic to the individual, presumed to be due to central nervous system dysfunction, and may occur across the life span" (National Center for Learning Disabilities 1997).

The definition also includes problems with social skills and emotional or behavioral disorders, but social and behavioral problems alone are not sufficient to warrant the diagnosis of a learning disability.

Individuals with Disabilities Education Act (IDEA) (PL 101-476, 1990)

IDEA provides a definition similar to the NJCLD's. In addition to the definition, terms such as perceptual disabilities, brain injury, minimal brain dysfunction, dyslexia, and developmental aphasia may apply. It does not include learning problems that are primarily the result of visual, hearing, or motor disabilities; mental retardation; or environmental, cultural, or economic disadvantage.

IDEA ——————————————————— Definition **4**

LD is a disorder of one or more of the basic psychological processes involved in understanding or in using spoken or written language, which may manifest itself in an imperfect ability to listen, think, speak, read, write, spell, or to do mathematical calculations.

Young children previously identified as having learning disabilities might be classified as having a developmental delay under the definitions in the reauthorized IDEA (1997). Children ages 3 through 8 may experience developmental delays in one or more of the following areas: physical, cognition, communication, social or emotional, or adaptive behaviors. Children with LD exhibit delays in one or more of these developmental areas, and school districts may elect to identify children in this age group who present with these characteristics under this exceptionality.

Prevalence . . . .

The number of people with learning disabilities cannot be accurately determined. Prevalence figures vary from researcher to researcher, organization to organization, and agency to agency. The lack of agreement on a definition of learning disabilities and the criteria for identification are the two most significant reasons for inconsistencies.

The National Institute of Health estimates that one in seven Americans, or about 15% of the U.S. population, has some type of learning disability ("Tell Me" 2000). Learning disabilities are commonly seen in families. There is a greater probability that a child will have LD if his parent(s) or grandparent(s) also has a learning disability. Most people with LD (approximately 80%) have reading problems; therefore, incidence figures often relate specifically to reading disabilities. Some studies report that approximately 5% of the school-aged population has LD, but other studies indicate that figure may be as many as 12% of all students.

Researchers estimate that 8-15% of the school population has learning disabilities in written expression, and 6% of the school population has difficulties in mathematics (Lyon 1996). Information from the National Center for Learning Disabilities (NCLD 1997) states that adolescents who have LD are at an increased risk for substance abuse, and as many as 60% of adolescents in substance abuse treatment programs have LD. The NCLD further reports that 35% of students with LD do not complete high school and that almost 65% of students with LD were not employed full-time one year after graduation from high school (1999). As many as 60% of adults with severe literacy problems have learning disabilities that were not identified or treated (NCLD 1999).

Etiology . . . .

Biological

Factors that interrupt the early development of the brain may cause a child to be born with pervasive developmental disabilities. Interruptions that occur later when the brain is becoming more specialized may appear as learning disorders. Advances in medical technology (e.g., position emission tomography [PET], magnetoencephalography [MEG], functional magnetic resonance imaging [fMRI]), and genetic analyses lead many scientists and physicians to link neurological and genetic factors to learning disabilities and attention deficit disorders (ADD). Structural and physiological differences have been investigated and differences have been found in individuals with learning disabilities and ADD.

Learning Disabilities

The National Institute for Mental Health (NIMH) reports several factors that affect normal brain development. Genetic factors such as chromosomes 15 and 6 may explain why learning disabilities, especially reading disorders, are more prevalent in families where dyslexia exists. Researchers at the Yale University School of Medicine also found differences in brain activation patterns of readers with dyslexia when compared with those of nondyslexic readers ("Biological Basis" 1998). The Yale researchers found that nondyslexic readers increased their brain activation in direct relation to the complexity of the reading task. The readers with dyslexia did not show a similar increase in brain activity. The disruptions occur in a posterior region of the brain (angular gyrus) responsible for making the visual and language associations necessary for reading.

Infections contracted by the mother during pregnancy and complications during delivery may impair the child's brain function and may also contribute to learning disabilities. The mother's use of tobacco, alcohol, and drugs such as cocaine, affect the developing fetus's brain. Children of mothers who smoke cigarettes or crack, or who consume alcohol or drugs are at greater risk for learning problems. Some of the risk factors include low birth weight (LBW) (less than 2500g), mental and growth retardation, respiratory illnesses, fetal alcohol syndrome, drug addiction at birth, hyperactivity, and physical deformities. Children who are exposed to or consume certain toxins, such as cadmium and lead, are at a greater risk for developing learning difficulties. The NIMH reports a growing body of evidence that learning problems can develop in young children with cancer who are treated with chemotherapy (Neuwirth 1993). Investigations into the social and academic learning disorders of children with known genetic syndromes such as Fragile X and Turner's syndrome are also being conducted (McElgunn 1996).

Attention Deficit Disorder (ADD)

Researchers at Emory University School of Medicine compared the neural activity of a control group of men without attention deficit disorder with an experimental group of adult men identified as having ADD with hyperactivity (ADHD). In the ADHD subjects, brain activity was more scattered and occurred primarily in the occipital region, an area associated with visual processing (Iskowitz 1998). The researchers believe that the inefficient use of this region of the brain explains why individuals with ADHD have deficits in working memory (the ability to store and retrieve information for a short period of time). Working memory is associated with the prefrontal region of the cortex.

Scientists at Stanford University investigated brain functioning and the effect of Ritalin on the brains of children with and without ADD. Boys between the ages of 8 and 13 played a game (pressed a button when they saw any letter of the alphabet except the letter X) while in a magnetic resonance imaging (MRI) device. The scientists were interested in imaging the frontal portions of the brain, including the frontal-lobe cortex and the striatal structures below it. The researchers found a difference in the activation of neuronal tissue in two structures in the striatal region, a region involved in motor control. They found further significant differences when the subjects performed the same activity after taking Ritalin. Both groups' motor and impulse control improved. The boys with ADD had more activity in the striatal structures, and the control group had less activity in those areas when taking Ritalin. The researchers concluded that the frontal striatal portion of the brain is linked to ADD, and that Ritalin impacts the functioning of the striatum ("Differences" 1998).

Discrepancy

Scientists and educators do not agree about the etiology of learning disabilities. Research findings are often contradictory and inconclusive. As a result, some professionals prefer to *describe* rather than label or classify the disorders. Those who use this method to identify people with LD cite the existence of a discrepancy among behaviors. In other words, the person with LD does not perform up to his ability. A discrepancy exists between the ability to perform and his aptitude. A person with a learning disability, by definition, has normal intelligence but exhibits significant difficulties in the acquisition and use of listening, speaking, reading, writing, reasoning, or mathematical abilities. One expects that a person with normal intelligence would develop and demonstrate age- and grade-level appropriate skills. People with learning disabilities exhibit delays and deficits in one or more areas of normal development. People who use the discrepancy method to describe LD likely cite unknown causes as the etiology of the disorder.

Types of Learning Disorders . . . .

Learning disabilities is not always a single disorder. Multiple disorders may occur at the same time. LD affects a person's ability to speak, listen, read, write, spell, reason, remember, organize information, and compute. The disabilities should not be confused with others that have similar conditions such as mental retardation, pervasive developmental disabilities, behavioral disorders, etc. The academic difficulties children with learning disabilities demonstrate are not directly related to their lack of educational opportunities, inadequate instruction, cultural differences, or economic disadvantages.

As you read *The Source for Learning Disabilities*, it's important to remember that many characteristic behaviors associated with learning disabilities are seen in *all* people. As you read, you will probably recognize some characteristics and behaviors in yourself. The significance of behaviors is determined by *how many* of the behaviors are present, and the *impact* they have on social interactions, academic progress, and vocational success.

Here are the major learning disabilities we will discuss in *The Source for Learning Disabilities* and some brief descriptions.

Communication Disorders • an impairment in the ability to receive, send, process, and comprehend concepts or verbal, nonverbal, and graphic symbol systems ("Definitions" 1993). Difficulties can occur in the areas of hearing, speech, and language.

Dyslexia • a disability that prohibits the acquisition and processing of language. Difficulties occur in reading, writing, spelling, handwriting, and mathematics. Dyslexia is a generic term that applies to individuals with all types of reading difficulties.

Dysgraphia • a disability that affects the ability to express oneself in writing (e.g., to form letters, to generate content, to revise, or to edit). People with generalized writing problems are often identified as having dysgraphia.

Dyscalculia • a mathematical disability whereby a person has difficulty understanding math concepts such as one-to-one correspondence, measurements of time and space, calculating number problems, or reasoning and solving word problems.

Attention Deficit Disorder (ADD) • is a consistent pattern of inattention that occurs more frequently and severely than in children at a similar level of development (DSM-IV 1994). ADD and LD often occur together, but the two disorders are not synonymous, and one disorder can be present in the absence of the other.

Dual Exceptionalities ·

There are dual exceptionalities to consider: gifted with learning disabilities and bilingual with disabilities. We want to briefly talk about these exceptionalities because they are often neglected in general LD reference books.

Gifted with Learning Disabilities

Students whose intellectual abilities exceed their academic performance may have LD. These students may be labeled underachievers, unmotivated, or even lazy. Yet they may have a dual exceptionality—gifted with learning disabilities. It's difficult to accurately identify gifted with LD students because they often use their intelligence to conceal the disability. For example, a student with a writing disability may engage in a verbal debate with the teacher rather than write an essay. A student with a reading problem may execute problem-solving behavior by delegating passages to members of his reading group in order to reduce the amount of reading he would have to complete.

Gifted students with learning disabilities often:

- employ abstract reasoning
- demonstrate exceptional mathematical reasoning ability
- have excellent visual memory and visual spatial skills
- possess large expressive and receptive vocabularies
- reveal a mature sense of humor
- use imagination and creativity
- demonstrate difficulty with memorization, computation, phonics, and/or spelling
- are distractible and disorganized
- daydream in specific situations due to boredom
- lack tolerance for working on tasks that seem irrelevant
- possess unreasonable personal expectations, may be hypersensitive, and perfectionist
- display an excellent use and understanding of abstract language
- exhibit a wide range of interests
- engage in power struggles with authorities
- question rules, customs and traditions

Bilingual with Learning Disabilities

More than 79 million school-aged children have limited English proficiency (LEP) or are bilingual. The U.S. Office of Special Education estimates that almost one million of these students have disabilities. Because of their language differences, many of these children are not identified. They are placed in bilingual educational settings and are not provided appropriate special education services (Baca and Cervantes 1991).

Accurate assessment of a child's strengths and weaknesses must first be undertaken. Standardized educational assessment instruments typically used to assess students suspected of having learning problems may not be valid or reliable indicators of these children's functioning levels. Non-standardized measurements (e.g., ecological inventories, portfolio assessments) along with the use of interpreters and translators provide a more accurate assessment of the functional abilities of children who have LEP or who are bilingual.

There are four categories of difficulties often identified in students who have LEP and learning problems (Root 1994). Many of the behaviors are also seen in individuals with learning disabilities but who are not bilingual.

1. Word-Retrieval Difficulties

Bilingual students with word-retrieval difficulties:

- volunteer to answer a question, but don't know the information when called on
- provide inaccurate sequential information (e.g., telling a story or giving verbal directions)
- rely on "forgetfulness" to mask word-finding difficulties
- delay starting tasks due to organizational difficulties
- acquire phonics and decoding skills slowly
- recall math facts slowly and execute calculations slowly

2. Attention Deficits

Bilingual students with attention deficits:

- have variable performance relative to number of people, and visual and auditory distractions
- attend to tasks inconsistently
- appear disoriented or confused due to language barrier
- delay responses in order to process information or to gain information from the environment
- fidget, daydream, and wander because they cannot follow instructions or complete tasks

3. Visual Association Deficits

Bilingual students with visual association deficits:

- struggle to complete problem-solving tasks, especially higher-level mathematics
- attend to irrelevant details
- don't understand inferential readings
- misuse or omit capital letters and punctuation marks
- ignore significant structural organizational features (e.g., italicized words and words written in bold type, headings with subheadings, map legends, etc.)

4. Organization and Self-Monitoring Problems

Bilingual students with organization and self-monitoring problems:

- rely on concrete information and reasoning
- offer few alternatives when solving problems
- use one dominant learning style even when unsuccessful
- predict outcomes and consequences poorly

Educators who work with children with LEP and children suspected of having a disability must consider three factors: the severity of the disability, the person's proficiency in the primary language (and in English), and the person's intelligence. Placement decisions for the bilingual exceptional student should reflect the accommodations for the type and nature of instruction to be provided, the language of instruction, and the student's learning needs and style.

Summary . . . .

Learning disabilities (LD) is a heterogeneous disorder that describes a variety of problems. People with learning disabilities can have problems in one or more of the following areas: psycho-social, communication, reading, writing, math, and attention. It's difficult to estimate the number of people who have learning disabilities because of lack of agreement over its definition and criteria for identification. Etiology of learning disabilities and attention deficit disorder has been attributed to neurological differences, but the debate continues over the true cause of the disorders.

Dual exceptionalities such as gifted with LD and bilingual with LD may also occur. To some degree or another, everyone identifies with characteristics associated with LD: disorganization, memory deficits, poor reading comprehension, spelling errors, frustration, and inadequate abstract math reasoning. The difference is in the impact the difficulties have on a person's social and emotional development, academic progress, and vocational success.

References and Resources . . . .

Baca, L. M. and Cervantes, H. T., "Bilingual Special Education," *ERIC Digest #496*, 1991, <http://www.ldonline.org/ld_indepth/bilingual_ld/esl_ld_eric.html> (June 26, 2000).

"Biological Basis for Reading Disability Discovered," *Proceedings of the National Academy of Sciences*, 1998, <http://www.ldonline.org/whats_new/biobasis.html> (May 2, 2000).

"Definition of Dyslexia," General Membership Meeting of the International Dyslexia Association Annual Conference, Internal Dyslexia Association, Los Angeles, CA, 1994.

"Definitions of Communication Disorders and Variations," *American Speech-Language-Hearing Association*, Vol. 35, Suppl. 10, 1993, pp. 40-41.

"Diagnostic and Statistical Manual for Mental Disorders, 4th Ed.," (DSM-IV), American Psychiatric Association, Washington, DC, 1994.

"Differences in Brain Function Found for Attention Deficit Disorder," 1998, <http://www.stanford.edu/dept/news/relaed/981123add-h.html> (March 17, 2000).

"How Can Research on the Brain Inform Education?" *Classroom Compass*, 3(2), Winter, 1997, <http://www.sedl.org/scimath/compass/v03n02/brain.html>, (May 2, 2000).

Iskowitz, M., "Neuro-Imaging Reveals a Physiological Correlate of Attention Deficit Hyperactivity Disorder," *Advance for Speech-Language Pathologists and Audiologists*, 8(29), 1998, pp. 7-9.

Lyon, G. R., "Learning Disabilities: Special Education for Students with Disabilities," *The Future of Children*, 6(1), Spring, 1996, <http://www.ldonline.org/ld_indepth/general_info/future/children.html> (May 2, 2000).

McElgunn, B., "Critical Discoveries in Learning Disabilities: A Summary of Findings by NIH Research Programs in Learning Disabilities," *Research Centers Report at the LDA 1996 Conference*, 1996, <http://www.ldanatl.org/newsbriefs/ju196/mcelgunn.html>, (March 18, 1999).

Mosby Medical, Nursing, and Allied Health Dictionary, 4th Ed., Mosby, St. Louis, MO, 1994.

National Center for Learning Disabilities, *Information about Learning Disabilities*, 1997, <http://www.ncld.org/ld/info_ld.html> (March 18, 1999).

National Center for Learning Disabilities, *General Information Packet on Learning Disabilities*, <http://www.ncld.org/brochures/geninfo.html> (May 13, 2000).

Neuwirth, S., "Learning Disabilities," National Institute of Mental Health, Washington, D.C., 1993.

"Primer on IDEA 1997 and Its Regulations," *CEC Today: Newsletter of the Council for Exceptional Children*, 5(7), April/May, 1999., <http://www.ldonline.org/ ld_indepth...ial_education/cec_idea_primer.html> (March 21, 2000).

Root, C., "A Guide to Learning Disabilities for the ESL Classroom Practitioner," *TESL-Electronic Journal*, Vol. 1(1), 1994, <http://www.ldonline.org/ ld_indepth/bilin-gual_ld/ esl_ld.html> (June 26, 2000).

Sousa, D. A., "Is the Fuss About Brain Research Justified?," 1998, <http://www.edweek.org/ew/vol-18/16sousa.h18> (May 2, 2000).

"Tell Me the Facts About Learning Disabilities," <http://www.ldonline.org/ ccldinfo/1.html> (June 26, 2000).

Turnbull, A., Turnbull, R., Shank, M., and Leal, D., *Exceptional Lives: Special Education in Today's Schools, 2nd Ed.*, Merrill, Upper Saddle River, NJ, 1999.

Webb, J. T. and Latimer, D., "ADHD and Children Who are Gifted," *ERIC Digest #522*, <http://www.ldonline.org/ld_indepth_adhd/eric522.html> (June 26, 2000).

Willard-Holt, C., "Dual Exceptionalities," *ERIC EC Digest #E574*, May 1999, <http://www.ldonline.org/ld_indepth/gt_ld/ericE574.html> (June 26, 2000).

■ ■

2

Social and Emotional Aspects of LD

Wesley is concerned about Patricio, a popular thirteen-year old, whom he tutors for math. Sometimes Patricio is outgoing and full of fun when he comes to the tutoring sessions. Other times he's withdrawn and sullen. He's down-right unpleasant to be around on some occasions. Wesley realizes that Patricio's erratic behavior began about the time he entered seventh grade at a new junior high school. Wesley wonders if Patricio could be uncomfortable at the new school because of his learning disability in math. For the first time, Patricio is having to succeed in a regular math class without benefit of the resource teacher who supported him in elementary school. Could this be frustrating and embarrassing him?

Wesley is probably correct in his speculation. Although Patricio is usually extroverted and positive, he could be experiencing social and emotional difficulties as a result of his math disability. Dealing with learning disabilities is never easy, and problems can be compounded by factors such as transitions to new schools and adolescent hormonal changes. With understanding and patience, parents and professionals can help Patricio achieve his highest potential and help him enjoy his teenage years.

Learning and Affective Problems

When a student has both learning and affective (i.e., social and emotional) difficulties, it's sometimes hard to determine if the primary problem is a learning disability or a social or emotional problem. Students with learning disabilities may develop affective problems that are either directly related to the characteristics of the disability, accompany it, or are a result of the learning disability. This is complicated by the fact that the noticeable characteristics of the disability may appear to change over time in relation to new demands put on students in new situations (Manganello 1992).

Recent brain and behavior research show profound relationships between thinking and feeling. Conditions once considered emotional are now believed to have a biological basis, and vice versa. It's not always simple or even desirable to differentiate between the two. Medication that alters neurotransmitter functioning allows some people to function better. Behavior modification and psychotherapy can also be effective. Therefore, professionals should consider a learning disability before they diagnose emotional or social disorders (Cicci 1995). Environmental stresses may also contribute to problems (Walker 1987).

Social, emotional, and cognitive development interact with verbal and nonverbal learning. For example, children with learning disabilities such as speech and language disorders have an increased risk of psychiatric problems. Likewise, children with psychiatric disorders are more likely to have speech and language disorders. Preschool children with speech and language problems are at risk for learning difficulties in first grade (Cicci 1995).

Social and Emotional Difficulties

Social and/or emotional difficulties can range from very mild to severe. Some students may be:

- embarrassed by poor grades
- overly-anxious about test scores
- upset because of communication difficulties with peers
- frustrated because of unrealistic expectations
- angry about the large amounts of time needed to do schoolwork
- despondent about exclusion from extracurricular activities
- depressed because of feelings of failure and hopelessness
- overly critical of themselves and others
- vulnerable to perfectionism to cope with anxiety
- tempted to give up

Academic Problems

Academic failure, in itself, can lead to affective difficulties. Being placed in special classes, being singled out for tutoring, or having to repeat a grade can cause mental anguish and adjustment problems. Inappropriate family or peer reactions to problems in school can further hinder emotional and social health. Therefore, consider all possible factors when planning how to best help students make successful social and emotional adjustments.

All students with learning disabilities do *not* have serious affective problems. In fact, some of these students have very good emotional health and are gifted in social relationships. Students may be very positive and cheerful. They can display a delightful sense of humor and a fresh way of looking at life. They may be well-liked by adults and peers. Because of their disabilities, they may have great empathy for the difficulties of others. They can be very dedicated to their goals and display an inordinate amount of commitment to achieving them. In other words, don't assume that students will have social or emotional problems just because they have learning disabilities.

Characteristics ·

In this section, we'll examine some common areas, such as self-esteem, emotions, social relationships, behavior, resilience, and special problems adults with LD may face.

Self-Esteem

Self-esteem is the feelings and thoughts that people have about their own competence, worth, and ability to make a difference in the world. People with good self-esteem confront rather than flee challenges, learn from successes and failures, and treat themselves and others with respect (Brookes 1997). A far-reaching goal for all students should be to develop positive, realistic self-esteem.

According to ground-breaking work by Erickson, people go through predictable stages of social-emotional development (1963). Elementary-aged children must face the challenge of resolving conflict between feelings of industry (e.g., self-reliance, competency) and inferiority. If children experience success during these early school years, they will develop positive attitudes about themselves and their abilities. They will view themselves as competent and industrious. On the other hand, if they experience frustration and failure, they will feel inferior and incompetent.

Unfortunately, many children with learning disabilities do not experience success in elementary school. Being identified as learning disabled or special can negatively affect the self-image of some children. So these children are more likely to develop poor self-esteem and negative ideas about their capabilities. If these children do succeed, they are more likely to attribute their success to luck than to their own abilities.

Emotions

Students with learning disabilities often report anxiety. They feel stress because of the inconsistencies of their performance, the supreme exertion and diligence it takes not to make mistakes, the large amounts of time and effort it takes to perform academic tasks, their confusion and failures at school, etc.

Unbearable amounts of stress, ridicule, embarrassment, and other negative feelings can lead to avoidance behaviors. Avoidance behaviors may be interpreted by teachers or parents as laziness or lack of caring. In reality, these students care very much and are trying their hardest to succeed (Ryan 1994).

The frustration and anxiety that students feel may also result in anger. Students may vent their anger on teachers and parents. Many times, students control their anger all day at school and later in the safer home environment, they vent their anger on their mothers (or other trusted adults). This is confusing to adults who are desperately trying to help their child (Ryan 1994).

Students with learning disabilities may display other negative emotions, such as depression, lack of energy, and withdrawal. They may obscure their difficulties by making jokes, trying to please everyone, or becoming involved in too many activities. They may become over-critical or afraid to take necessary risks to learn and grow. Perfectionism, driving themselves too hard, discounting praise, and an inability to see small successes are other common characteristics. Some students (and parents) grieve over their disabilities and perceptions of lost opportunities. They may view the world and themselves negatively and be unable to imagine a positive future.

Social Relationships

Some students with learning disabilities have problems with social relationships. There are many reasons that might account for this.

Students with disabilities:

- may misinterpret emotions, moods, social cues, and inferences

- may have trouble interpreting nonverbal behavior such as body language, facial expressions, and socially-appropriate personal distance

- may have problems understanding humor

- may have less social knowledge (e.g., how to make friends, how to enter a game) or be unable to apply this knowledge

- may not have acquired the knowledge needed to participate in conversations with peers

- can spend so much time studying that they do not have time to develop normal social relationships

If students have communication disorders (i.e., hearing, speech, language, central auditory processing), communicating with others can be difficult. For example, students with **speech disorders** may be unable to easily produce understandable speech and may be reluctant to participate in oral conversations. Students with **hearing problems** may become confused when trying to follow conversations or may misarticulate speech sounds. Students with **language processing problems** such as dyslexia may have trouble remembering the right words or hesitate before answering questions. They might have trouble with pragmatic language (e.g., using language in different ways in different situations or with different people) or idiomatic language (e.g., puns, figures of speech). They may also get events out of sequence when trying to tell a joke or describe an event. These problems are especially detrimental in adolescence when language is crucial to good relationships with peers (Ryan 1994).

Poor self-esteem and negative emotions that can accompany learning disabilities can also be detrimental to social interactions. These attributes often lower confidence and keep students from making good impressions and enjoying social situations. A poor self-image, negative thoughts about one's capabilities, and pessimistic attitudes greatly hinder healthy relationships.

Research is conflicting as to how well students with learning disabilities are socially accepted by peers. In many situations, it may be that social acceptance is not influenced by the learning disability as much as the social climate created by teachers and parents (Heward and Orlansky 1988).

Behavior

There is contrary evidence regarding the relationship of learning disabilities and behavioral problems due to difficulty subtyping and differentiating learning disabilities, such as dyslexia and ADHD (Dickman 1996). However, there does seem to be support for the following:

1. Each learning disability subtype poses a unique and variable risk for abnormal development of prosocial behavior.

2. Co-occurrence of LD subtypes enhances the risk.

3. Environmental factors (e.g., school failure, low socioeconomic status) also enhance the risk.

Behaviors associated with learning disabilities are diverse. For example, some students may become class clowns to obtain attention and hide their disabilities. Others might pretend to be uninterested in class activities in order to avoid the possibility of failure. They might also be disruptive, aggressive, or misbehave in other ways as a result of negative feelings or to disguise their learning problems. Some students develop learned helplessness or the perception that they are powerless to control what happens to them.

The presence of learning disabilities can contribute to juvenile delinquency directly and indirectly through school failure. People may also react differently to individuals with learning disabilities. When many people with learning disabilities get into trouble, the same difficulties that cause problems with academic work cause problems when they try to explain themselves. Many times they look and act guilty even when they are not. Youths with learning disabilities are more likely to be arrested or receive sentencing than those without learning disabilities for similar offenses. They are also more likely to be trapped within the juvenile justice system (Crawford 1996).

Older students who seek employment in high school or college may have problems with finding and keeping a steady job. The world of work may make the learning disability more apparent or more incapacitating. Sometimes people with learning disabilities turn to substance abuse to cope or escape (Manganello 1992).

Resilience

Resilience is the ability to to recover from or adjust easily to misfortune or change. It's puzzling why some children with learning disabilities overcome their problems to be successful, well-adjusted adults, while others with similar disabilities continue to have problems. The following factors are important (Brookes 1997):

Temperament

Children who are resilient often have:

- easy-going temperments from birth, which elicit positive responses from caregivers
- more advanced problem-solving skills
- better coping strategies
- more appropriate social skills
- higher cognitive abilities than less-resilient children

Self-Esteem

Children who are resilient seem to have:

- better self-esteem
- a more realistic view of their own personal control
- a sense of hope
- the belief that they can overcome their problems, which can be self-fulfilling

Home Environment

Children who are resilient tend to have:

- positive, loving, supportive families
- homes with reasonable and clear structure and limits

Social Environment

Children are encouraged to develop resilience through:

- positive experiences with extended family, friends, community, school, and other social contacts
- the support of at least one caring adult who encourages them (e.g., parent, other family member, teacher, coach)

Possible affective problems can include:

- **low self-esteem**

- **negative emotions**

- **poor social relationships**

- **behavior problems**

- **lack of resilience**

On a whole, there is a lack of awareness of the social and emotional issues affecting adults with learning disabilities. It's not clear to what degree affective problems exist into adulthood. Some data suggests that many problems are transitory, that they cease to be a prominent concern when compulsory schooling ends, and that these children develop into well-adjusted adults (Bruck 1986; Reiff and Gerber 1995). In addition, social and emotional problems of adults appear to be widely distributed and not isolated to the individuals with the most severe learning disabilities (Bruck 1986).

In some cases, however, problems tend to persist and may even intensify in adulthood. Consider these diverse explanations (Reiff and Gerber 1995):

- **Adults** indicate that they sometimes experience **adjustment problems** in adulthood as a result of negative feelings, perceptions, and experiences caused by learning disabilities in childhood. For example, they report feeling stupid and unpopular when they were in school. Memories of school are still painful and affect feelings of self worth and competence, leading to anger or depression. Negative experiences can result in a self-perpetuating cycle of emotional liability and social failures. On the other hand, other adults can learn to use negative experiences as motivation to succeed. However, even successful adults often indicate carrying unwanted emotional baggage from childhood.

- **Adults** report that deficits in learning capabilities sometimes directly affect **social relationships**. For example, an adult who finds it difficult to remember important details might find it hard to participate in a conversation requiring memory for details. Adults who do not write well will probably be uncomfortable writing letters, memos, or notes to others. Adults who have not mastered basic math skills may become nervous when they have to calculate how to split a check in a restaurant with friends. Poor readers may avoid situations in which they may be asked to read aloud.

- **Adults** may find that they have missed out on learning needed **social skills** because they were in segregated special education settings as children. As a result, they did not have opportunities for typical social interactions with peers who were not disabled or they lacked common experiences upon which to base social interactions. Others report that they were too busy dealing with their disabilities to develop and practice normal social and emotional relationships with others.

- **Adults** report that social and emotional problems related to learning disabilities can also greatly interfere with **vocational success**, **personal relationships**, **leisure pursuits**, and **general well-being**. Fortunately, many adults have found ways to cope and compensate for their weaknesses. Most testify that a learning disability is not a doomsday sentence for healthy and happy relationships.

Screening ·

The checklist on pages 26-27 has feelings and behaviors that may indicate social or emotional problems that accompany a learning disability. There are many more that could be listed; any emotion or behavior that is troubling to students or is affecting their functioning in life should be taken seriously.

Keep in mind that the severity of a learning disability does not indicate the extent of the accompanying affective problem. For example, a mild case of dyslexia may seriously affect the life of a college student, or a mild speech problem in adolescence may contribute to significant mental anguish and isolation for a teenager. Psychiatric disorders such as mood disorders, anxiety disorders, tic disorders, and substance-related disorders may coexist with learning disabilities (Cicci 1995). Students *without* learning disabilities may have some of these characteristics as well.

Check the column that indicates the frequency of the directly observed or reported behavior. Tally the number and frequency that the behaviors occur. When red flags appear, immediately seek further diagnosis from mental health professionals familiar with learning disabilities. Early intervention is important—waiting can have serious and long-lasting consequences.

Social/Emotional Screening Checklist

Name_____

Seldom = S   Frequently = F   Always = A

Characteristic	S	F	A
poor self esteem/feelings of inferiority			
feelings of powerlessness			
unrealistic pressure and expectations			
unresolved grief associated with learning disabilities			
anger			
emotional anguish			
sorrow and pain			
excessive worrying/anxiety			
embarrassment/shame			
nervousness			
overly-critical of self/others			
perfectionist			
lack of energy; inertia			
little sense of satisfaction in accomplishments			
poor motivation or uncaring attitude			
emotional outbursts			
hopelessness			
instability or mood swings			
depression			
isolation or withdrawal			
unnatural fear of being wrong or failing			
over-avoidance of risk or refusal to try			
blaming others for problems			
credits others for successes, or attributes successes to luck			
bragging or bullying			
learned helplessness			

Social/Emotional
Screening Checklist, *continued*

Name_____

Seldom = S   Frequently = F   Always = A

Characteristic	S	F	A
little response to praise			
rebelliousness			
aggression/disruptive behavior			
class clown			
hyperactivity			
over-compensating and driving oneself too hard			
inability to bounce back from setbacks			
social or emotional immaturity			
preference for playing with younger children			
poor judgment of moods and feelings of others			
insensitivity to social contexts and cues			
inaccurate social perceptions			
inept at social problem solving			
problems interpreting facial expressions and nonverbal gestures			
difficulties communicating with others			
difficulties seeing points of view of others			
problems making/maintaining friendships			
discomfort or avoidance of social situations			
inappropriate remarks/actions in social situations			
rejection or ostracism by classmates			
persistent social/emotional adjustment problems			
denial of obvious social/emotional problems			
little adult support			
no area of excellence to boost confidence			
psychiatric problems (obsessive-compulsive disorder, eating disorder, etc.)			

Intervention . . . .

Students who develop good social and emotional health can successfully overcome or live with the effects of disabilities. A student with dyslexia who learns to read, a student with dyscalculia who becomes proficient at mathematics, or a student with ADHD who learns to sit still and pay attention to schoolwork are examples of individuals who can be proud of themselves and their accomplishments.

In addition to helping students learn to read, do math, or pay attention, parents and educators should work together to help students build self-esteem, experience positive emotions, and have healthy interpersonal relationships. They can also help students control behaviors and build resilience to life's setbacks.

Intervention Strategies . . . .

Use the strategies in this section as starting points in assisting students. Thoughtfully consider what works and what does not, then modify and add to the strategies to fit your students' individual needs. If your help is not enough, the last section will give you some ideas on how to help students and their families obtain additional assistance.

Classroom Environment

Don't underestimate the effects of a proper social and emotional climate in encouraging or discouraging positive affective development.

Provide a Safe Classroom Atmosphere

- Foster a classroom atmosphere of trust, cooperation, compassion, and risk-taking.

- Model positive attitudes, helpful conversation, and constructive actions.

- Do not permit ridicule, sarcasm, or superiority to exist in your classroom.

- Give students opportunities to share their experiences with each other.

- Help others to view your students positively and to treat them well.

- If you promote healthy relationships and value all students, your students will learn to do the same.

Consider Students' Learning Styles

- Provide a suitable physical environment (e.g., lighting, temperature, appropriate amount of stimulation).

- Set appropriate goals and timelines.

- Use proper teaching techniques and materials so all students can perform to the best of their abilities.

- If students are actively learning and happily involved in school, many affective problems can be avoided or ameliorated.

Limit Study Time

- Students need time to relax, rest, play, and participate in extracurricular activities to avoid burn-out and social/emotional problems.

- Modify tasks so the volume of work and the time involved is manageable.

- Work with parents to limit the amount of time students are allowed to spend studying each day.

Use Multiple Resources

- Read and discuss books about people with diverse disabilities and talents, problems similar to those your students face, positive and negative emotions, and social relationships.

- Use videos and songs that express emotions and describe situations your students can identify with as springboards for discussion.

Carefully Consider Placement Options

- Carefully consider educational, emotional, and social effects of placement options (e.g., full or partial inclusion in regular class, self-contained, or resource special education).

- Thoughtfully work with students, their families, and other professionals to make good decisions regarding a placement.

- Be flexible and make changes when a placement is not effective or proves detrimental.

- No two students are alike—even students with similar disabilities may profit from different placements.

- Wherever students are placed, make sure educators understand the students, value them, and have the resources to help them.

The Source for Learning Disabilities
Copyright © 2000 LinguiSystems, Inc.

Self-Esteem

Healthy self-esteem is necessary for mental health and for satisfying personal relationships. Try the following strategies to build your students' self-esteem.

Self-Awareness and Confidence

- Help students become self-aware and realistically see themselves as complex individuals with strengths and weaknesses.

- Assist students in understanding their disabilities and the resulting effects on their lives.

- Show students how to build on strengths and compensate for weaknesses.

- Help students see how their disabilities can actually lead them to discover hidden talents. For example, a child who finds it difficult to read aloud might have a gift for oral storytelling.

- Teach problem-solving skills. Students will be more likely to develop good self-esteem if they view themselves as capable of making decisions and resolving problems.

Developing Identity

- Help each student develop a sense of identity.

- Have students make timelines of their lives. Include obviously important events (e.g., birth dates, first school year) and events that are not so obvious but important to individual students (e.g., date a beloved pet died, etc.).

- Have students write or draw autobiographies, using their timelines as guides.

- Help students appreciate individual differences in themselves and in others.

Responsibility and Goals

- Provide students with reasonable responsibilities and choices. This will help them develop a feeling of competence and healthy pride.

- Help students set attainable goals and provide experiences for them to succeed.

- Guide students to keep visible records of their progress, such as a posted chart, private checklist, or success journal.

Making Mistakes

- Guide your students to realize that it is okay to make mistakes. Model and teach them to accept and learn from mistakes.

- Emphasize improvement rather than perfection.

Areas of Excellence

- Help students find at least one area of excellence.

- Give them opportunities to succeed at sports, art, cooking, tutoring, computers, video games, and other activities.

- Make sure students have time and other resources to pursue areas of excellence.

- Provide activities that require different talents and skills, such as cooperative groups in which students have different jobs (e.g., recorder, artist, calculator).

Students Can Help Others

- Encourage students to share their knowledge and gifts.

- Provide opportunities for students to help others. They might participate in activities like these:

  ✔ read or tell stories to younger children
  ✔ show others how to use technology (e.g., calculators, computers, camcorders)
  ✔ work on a community service project (e.g., food bank, homeless shelter)
  ✔ house-sit or care for a pet for neighbors on vacation
  ✔ get an elderly person's mail for him/her
  ✔ prepare a simple meal for an over-worked parent
  ✔ help coach younger children in a favorite sport
  ✔ volunteer to work at a summer camp

Praise and Appreciation

- Encourage students and give specific, sincere praise.

- Value students' interests and talents.

- Ask questions and show enthusiasm.

- Avoid false compliments; most students are aware when praise is undeserved.

- If older students are embarrassed by praise or encouragement given out in front of others, do so in private.

- Teach students to praise each other sincerely. Some teachers have students record what they appreciate about each other and share. Monitor this so all students are recognized positively and equally.

Inspiration

- Teach students about others who have overcome difficulties in life.

- Provide books, audiotapes, and videos on famous people who have overcome adversities.

- Talk about people you encounter in daily life who have conquered fears and problems.

- Share your own difficulties and how you have handled them, if appropriate.

Emotions

Negative emotions can sap energy and rob students of motivation. Model and encourage emotional health.

Expressing Emotions

- Encourage students to talk about their feelings to you and to trusted friends.

- Actively listen and observe body language and facial expressions.

- Know what feelings and perceptions are typical and atypical for students' age groups so you can recognize disparities.

- Realize that students with learning disabilities may have difficulties communicating their ideas and emotions.

- Teach students to recognize and label their feelings. It's difficult for them to talk about emotions if they don't know what they are or what to call them.

- If students are hesitant to express emotions, encourage them to use puppets, costumes, dolls, role-playing, etc.

Negative Emotions

- Emphasize the importance of dealing with negative feelings, and help students find constructive things to do to help themselves feel better.

- Explain that everyone, even the brightest, most popular people, sometimes feel badly about themselves and their lives. They are not alone.

Keeping a Journal or Diary

- Encourage students to keep journals or diaries to record their thoughts and feelings.

- Allow students to vent negative emotions without fear of judgment or retribution.

- Let students know that their journal entries are confidential, and you will only read them if they ask you to do so. Respond to their journal feelings with positive comments and encouragement.

Attitudes and Stress

- Teach students to think optimistically. Their thoughts influence their emotions and their actions.

- Students might benefit from stress-management techniques, such as visualization and deep muscle relaxation.

- Encourage good nutrition and adequate rest and exercise to reduce stress.

- Appreciate your students. People who feel appreciated are more likely to have good emotional health.

Social

Students enjoy and need good interpersonal relationships, which is especially true during adolescence.

Communication Skills

- Teach students effective communication skills.

- Help students know how to use verbal and nonverbal language.

- Provide practice in simulated and real-life situations.

Social Situations

- Analyze and talk about social situations and how to handle them positively.

- Role-play with activities such as introducing oneself to a new friend, showing hospitality, giving and accepting compliments, and other common situations.

- Observations and videotapes can give students practice decoding social situations so they can deal with them.

- Watching television shows with the volume off can assist them in decoding nonverbal language.

- Teach when, why, and how to use social skills.

- Discussions, role-playing, and analysis alone are not enough. Provide students with opportunities to use social skills in everyday life. Then help them reflect on their experiences.

- Have students continue to review and use newly-learned skills so they will maintain and generalize them to unfamiliar situations.

Healthy Interactions

- Make sure students with learning disabilities are included with students without disabilities in common school situations.

- Provide class activities that require everyone to participate in a non-threatening manner.

- Group sing-alongs, plays with costumes, choral readings, group games, partner projects, and puppet shows can provide social interaction naturally.

- Arrange informal interactions during recess, lunch, extracurricular activities, and study groups.

- Respect each child's comfort zone regarding socializing to provide just the right amount of support and participation.

- If necessary, take steps to see that students with disabilities are not isolated or treated differently during these social times.

Friendships

- Be alert for opportunities to help students develop real friendships with peers with and without disabilities.

- Encourage parents to let students invite friends over, talk on the phone, and engage in other typical activities.

- If friendships do not come easily, you may need to work with families to provide structured activities through which friendships can develop (e.g., clubs, sporting events, planned outings).

- Teach students to choose friends and social activities wisely. Discuss characteristics and examples of good friendships. When students participate in healthy social activities, they are too busy to participate in unhealthy ones.

Behavior

Negative behaviors can be harmful to students with learning disabilities and affect everyone in the classroom. Take steps to positively guide students to interact appropriately.

Rules and Consequences

- Make sure the rules and expectations in your classroom are fair and impartial.

- Help students understand the reasons for rules.

- Let students help you formulate rules and consequences.

- Help students understand why they behave as they do.

- Guide students to find constructive ways to deal with their problems.

- Help students realize that they are responsible for their own actions.

Prevention

- Focus on prevention rather than punishment.

- Sometimes a change in environment facilitates more favorable behavior. For example, if a student becomes loud and agitated when taking a test with the class, give the test in a more restricted environment.

Encouraging Desired Behaviors

- Teach acceptable ways to behave and communicate. For example, if a student is angry, teach him/her how to express and deal with the anger by understanding the anger, writing in a journal, and engaging in physical exercise rather than hurting others or turning it inward.

- Help students anticipate the consequences of their behavior. "What if . . ." games can be helpful. For example, one student or the teacher poses a situation (e.g., What if I take Sandra's candy without asking?). Another student describes the consequence (e.g., Sandra will be angry and won't play with me anymore). Be sure to include positive behaviors and consequences (e.g., What if I ask Sandra to share her candy with me?).

- Analyze your students' challenging behaviors. Ask yourself:
    - ✔ What happened before the behavior?
    - ✔ What happened after the behavior?
    - ✔ Was the behavior rewarding for the student?
    - ✔ Is there any way to make sure that the behavior is unrewarding if it occurs again?
    - ✔ What are more constructive behaviors the student could replace this one with?

- Don't inadvertently provide reinforcement for challenging behaviors. Remember that many students regard negative attention as better than no attention.

- When appropriate, allow students to provide restitution for hurtful acts.

- Educate students about substance abuse. Help them learn coping mechanisms to alleviate the temptation to use tobacco, drugs, or alcohol to deal with problems.

Teach Students to Think Before They Act

- Teach students to count to ten; repeat a confirming, positive statement; or recite a silly rhyme before engaging in an impulsive behavior.

- Give them time to cool off and think rationally about their options. Praise self-discipline.

Learned Helplessness

- Help students avoid or overcome learned helplessness.

- Let them know that everyone is dependent on others sometimes.

- Help them see that there are aspects of their lives that they can control and many situations that they can make better.

- Encourage them to be as independent as possible.

Positive Feedback

- Show students how their behaviors can affect their feelings and self-esteem. Help them see that positive behaviors can help them feel good about themselves and others.

- Provide positive feedback and reinforcement for appropriate behaviors. Give small, tangible rewards if needed. Withdraw tangible rewards as appropriate behaviors become habitual.

- Praise students when they do something constructive or uplifting.

- Make a class game in which everyone is alert for peers who are especially helpful or thoughtful. Keep a box in which students insert anonymous slips of paper with the "caught-you" reports to be shared weekly. Be sure to include your own anonymous "caught-you" slips.

The Source for Learning Disabilities
Copyright © 2000 LinguiSystems, Inc.

A Safe Refuge

- Everyone needs a place to take refuge. Make sure students have a place to go in the classroom when they need time away from others and from activities.

- Encourage families to provide safe refuges at home.

Resilience

Resilient children are more likely to grow into happy, productive adults. The previous strategies that encourage children to build good self-esteem, practice positive behaviors, and develop good social relationships will help make them more resilient. Help develop resilience in these ways too:

- Believe in your students and help them deal positively with adversity.

- Guide students' families and friends to know the importance of supporting them and how to provide support.

- Teach students (and their families) to be their own advocates. Guide them to speak up and take constructive steps when they feel they are being treated unfairly or not receiving services to which they are entitled.

- As mentioned earlier, help students find an area in which they can excel. Do not withdraw participation from this activity as punishment for the effects of the learning disability (e.g., poor grades, more time needed to study).

- Help students realize that a certain amount of discomfort and risk is to be expected in life, and even positive change can be painful. Model and teach them to be confident and adaptive and to embrace challenges as opportunities to learn and grow.

Don't Go It Alone

The scope and breadth of problems are beyond the expertise of the classroom teacher sometimes. Know when and where to find help.

Don't Try to Handle All Problems by Yourself

- Educators and families should be in constant communication and consultation as to how to best help students.

- Let the family help you. When appropriate strategies are used at both school and home, they are more likely to be successful.

Keep a Resource List

- Keep a list of names and telephone numbers of mental health professionals; Web sites and telephone numbers of professional organizations; titles of books, videos, and journal articles; state and local agencies that can offer assistance; and support groups.

- Recommend your resource list to students and their families.

- Keep your list up-to-date by checking the numbers and addresses from time to time.

- Get feedback from families as to the helpfulness of each resource.

Support Groups and Treatment

- Encourage students and families to seek out appropriate support groups, if needed. Support groups can help students and their families deal with sensitive issues in positive ways. Many groups have a professional counselor who facilitates discussions.

- Share your knowledge about reputable, proven treatments with students and families. Help them avoid being taken advantage of by unscrupulous people promising quick fixes.

Crisis Management

- Intervene *before* a crisis occurs. Don't wait until problems become severe, incapacitating, or destructive.

- When students' problems are interfering with their lives, seek immediate help from families, counselors, psychologists, social workers, and professionals who are trained to deal with affective problems and have experience with individuals with learning disabilities.

- Know good crisis management procedures and your school district's guidelines.

- Know how to handle an emergency (e.g., student threatens to hurt himself or others) before it arises.

- Document and report all incidents to the appropriate personnel as soon as possible.

Summary . . . .

All students with learning disabilities do *not* have social and emotional problems. In fact, some students are gifted in these areas. However, when students with learning disabilities have social and emotional problems, it's necessary to ask if the primary problem is a learning disability or an affective problem.

Brain and behavior research show profound relationships between thinking and feeling. Conditions once considered emotional are now believed to have a biological basis and vice versa. Environmental stresses can further complicate matters. Students with learning disabilities can have difficulties with self-esteem, emotions, social relationships, and behavior. Students who are resilient are most likely to overcome their problems. For some adults, social and emotional problems are minimized when compulsory schooling ends. These problems may continue or intensify for others.

Students should be carefully screened, and intervention should occur before a crisis develops. Students should not be left to their own devices. Parents, educators, and mental health professionals should work together to find strategies and resources to assist students in developing social and emotional health and leading happy, productive lives.

References and Resources . . . .

Brookes, R., "Look What You've Done: Stories of Hope and Resilience," (Teacher's video guide), Greater Washington Educational Telecommunications Association, Inc., Washington, D.C., 1997.

Bruck, M., "Social and Emotional Adjustments of Learning Disabled Children: A Review of the Issues," In Ceci, S. (Ed.), *Handbook of Cognitive, Social, and Neuro-Psychological Aspects of Learning Disabilities*, Vol. I, Lawrence Erlbaum Associates, London, 1986, pp. 361-80.

Cicci, R., *What's Wrong with Me?*, Baltimore Press, New York, 1995.

Crawford, D., "Review of Research on Learning Disabilities and Juvenile Delinquency," In Cramer, S. and Ellis, W. (Eds.), *Learning Disabilities: Lifelong Issues*, Brookes, Baltimore, 1996.

Dickman, G., "The Link Between Learning Disabilities and Behavior," In Cramer, S. and Ellis, W. (Eds.), *Learning Disabilities: Lifelong Issues*, Brookes, Baltimore, 1996.

Erikson, E., *Childhood and Society*, W. W. Norton, New York, 1963.

Heward, W. and Orlansky, M., *Exceptional Children*, Merill, Columbus, OH, 1988.

Levine, M., *All Kinds of Minds*, Educator's Publishing Service, Cambridge, 1994.

Manganello, R., "Psychosocial Problems Among Learning Disabled College Students," *Research and Teaching in Developmental Education*, 9(1), 1992, pp. 67-78.

Pearl, R., "Social Cognitive Factors in Learning-Disabled Children's Social Problems," In Ceci, S. (Ed.), *Handbook of Cognitive, Social, and Neuropsychological Aspects of Learning Disabilities*, Vol. II, Lawrence Erlbaum Associates, London, 1987, pp. 273-294.

Reiff, H. and Gerber, P., *Learning Disabilities in Adulthood*, ProEd, Austin, TX, 1995.

Ryan, M., "The Other Sixteen Hours," International Dyslexia Association, Baltimore, MD, 1994.

Vail, P., *Emotion: The On-Off Switch for Learning*, Modern Learning Press, Rosemont, 1994.

Walker, E., "Commentary: Socioemotional Factors in Learning Disabilities," In Ceci, S. (Ed.), *Handbook of Cognitive, Social, and Neuropsychological Aspects of Learning Disabilities*, Lawrence Erlbaum Associates, London, 1987, pp. 295-298.

. . . .

Notes

. . . .

3

Communication Disorders

Darnell, a 6th grader, nervously awaits his turn as the teacher calls on students to answer questions about last night's homework. Whenever she calls on him to answer, he has a hard time quickly finding the words he wants to say. Everyone in class tries to answer for him. How embarrassing. He's good at answering questions on multiple choice tests. He wishes he could answer *all* the teacher's questions by taking multiple-choice tests. Then he wouldn't have to talk.

Communication is a social and cognitive process composed of gestural, oral, and graphic symbols. Social interaction happens when people express their wants, feelings, thoughts, and ideas. Concepts and information are acquired, understood, and expressed by touching, gesturing, listening, speaking, reading, and writing. People with learning disabilities frequently have difficulty with the reception and/or expression of one or more of the symbol systems required for effective communication. There are many children like Darnell—kids who have difficulty correctly speaking or expressing their ideas, or comprehending what they hear or read.

This chapter outlines the different types of communication disorders, discusses the incidence of specific types, and provides a checklist to help identify hearing, speech, or language disorders. You'll also find general intervention strategies.

Definition . . . .

The American-Speech-Language-Hearing Association (ASHA) defines a communication disorder as an *impairment in the ability to receive, send, process, and comprehend concepts or verbal, nonverbal, and graphic symbol systems* ("Definitions" 1993).

A communication disorder may:

- be evident in a hearing, language, and/or speech process
- range in severity from mild to profound
- be developmental or acquired
- be demonstrated by one or more communication of disorders
- result in a primary disability or be secondary to other disabilities

The significance of a communication disorder depends on:

- whether the disorder is developmental or acquired
- the number and type of disorder
- the ease with which a person can correctly produce speech sounds or learn to apply compensatory communication strategies
- the impact the disorder has on expression and/or reception of speech and language
- accompanying disorders (e.g., learning disability, developmental disabilities)

Incidence

The National Institute on Deafness and Other Communication Disorders (NIDCD) estimates that 46 million people in the U.S. have some type of communication disorder. Of these, approximately 14 million have a speech, voice, or language disorder. More than 28 million Americans have some type of hearing disorder (Castrogiovanni 2000). The remaining number have "other" communication disorders, which include more than one type of hearing, speech, and language disorder.

Ten percent of children younger than eight have a speech or language disorder (LDonline 1999). Disorders involving the production of speech sounds occur most frequently in children. Approximately 10% of the preschool and school-aged children have phonological disorders (Castrogiovanni 2000). The relationship between phonological disorders and subsequent reading, writing, spelling, and math abilities is significant (Castrogiovanni 2000). The Diagnostic and Statistical Manual of Mental Disorders-IV (DSM-IV) reports that 3-5% of children may have an expressive language disorder, and about 1% of the school-aged population are children who stutter (1994). Incidence of communication disorders is greater when there is a family history of similar or related communication disorders. Males generally have more communication disorders than females.

Categories of Communication Disorders

There are three major categories of communication disorders: hearing, speech, and language. They are explained fully on pages 46-53.

Hearing Disorders

Hearing disorders result from an impairment in the auditory system (i.e., the sensory pathways and the outer, middle, and inner ear). A hearing disorder may limit the development, comprehension, production, and maintenance of speech and language.

The terms *deaf* and *hard of hearing* are directly related to degree of hearing loss. A person who is deaf has a severe hearing loss (+70 dB) which significantly limits the use of the auditory channel for speech and language development with or without amplification. Someone identified as hard of hearing has a moderate to severe hearing loss (+30 dB-70 dB), which impacts the normal development of speech and language to varying degrees. Most people who are deaf and hard of hearing have communication disorders. Severity of the communication disorder increases as the degree of hearing loss increases.

A hearing loss can directly affect learning and academic achievement, but a learning disability "may be diagnosed in the presence of such sensory deficits only if the learning difficulties are in excess of those usually associated with these deficits" ("Diagnostic" 1994). In other words, if the hearing loss is the primary reason a person is not developing, using, and understanding language symbols, then that person's primary exceptionality is hearing impairment. There are three types of hearing disorders we'll discuss here: conductive, sensori-neural, and mixed.

Conductive Hearing Loss

Conductive hearing loss is marked by:

- an abnormality in the outer or middle ear

- difficulty perceiving speech sounds correctly

- a perceived loss of volume

- a temporary condition (e.g, fluid behind the eardrum) that can be generally treated with medications

- a permanent condition (i.e., scarring of the eardrum) that may require the person to use an assistive listening device or hearing aid

Sensori-Neural Hearing Loss

Sensori-neural hearing loss is marked by:

- an abnormality involving the inner ear or the sensory pathways that lead to the brain

- a congenital loss with an etiology that is hereditary or unknown

- exposure to loud noises, such as gunfire, car engines, and loud music

- the aging process (i.e., presbycusis)

- difficulty understanding sounds regardless of the volume

- a permanent loss

- amplification depending on severity of loss

- a recommendation of speech and language therapy for young children, especially during the period for speech and language development (i.e., birth-three years)

- an alternative mode of communication for severe congenital losses (e.g., sign language)

- a possible need for special education

Mixed Hearing Loss

Mixed hearing loss is marked by:

- a combined conductive and sensori-neural loss

- difficulty hearing and understanding sounds

- the nature and severity of loss determines primary course of treatment and intervention

- a possible need for medical intervention, amplification, and speech and language therapy

Speech Disorders

Speech disorders include impairments in articulation, fluency, and voice. These impairments involve the production of voice and speech sounds. Word meaning is not associated with speech disorders.

Articulation

An articulation disorder is marked by:

- omissions, substitutions, distortions, or additions of speech sounds

- errors that persist beyond the period associated with young children's speech development

- the inability to easily produce the sound correctly without intervention

Voice

A voice impairment is marked by:

- the abnormal production and/or the absence of vocal quality, pitch, loudness, resonance, or duration

- the inappropriate use or misuse of the voice (e.g., shouting, talking loudly)

- a medical condition (e.g., upper respiratory infections, allergies, laryngeal cancer)

- an abnormal vocal quality which may sound harsh, hoarse, breathy, or tense

- an inappropriately high- or low-pitched voice that occurs beyond puberty

- difficulty controlling the duration or amount of speech produced on one exhalation (e.g., people with developmental or progressive central nervous system disorders such as cerebral palsy and Parkinson's disease)

- variations in vocal pitch and loudness indicative of poor respiratory-phonatory control or a hearing loss

The Source for Learning Disabilities
Copyright © 2000 LinguiSystems, Inc.

- an abnormal resonance (e.g., hypernasality and hyponasality) associated with cleft palate or nasal obstructions. (Too much or too little air escapes into the nasal cavity making the voice sound hypernasal or hyponasal.)

- vocal characteristics that are inconsistent with the person's age, gender, or physical characteristics

Fluency

A fluency disorder is marked by:

- an abnormal rate and rhythm of speech

- an interruption in the flow of speech (stuttering) is characterized by repetitions, blocking, and prolongations of sounds, syllables, words, and phrases

- excessive tension, struggle, or other secondary characteristics (e.g., facial and bodily tension and movement)

- rapid, dysrhythmic, sporadic, unorganized, and frequently unintelligible speech (i.e., cluttering). Accelerated speech is not always present, but an impairment in formulating language is almost always present (Daly 1996).

Language Disorders

A person with a learning disability has a language disorder, which is why some professionals use the term *language-learning disabilities* (LLD). Language disorders include impairments in comprehension and expression of gestural, spoken, and written language symbol systems. Language disorders have three major components: *form* (phonology, morphology, syntax), *content* (semantics), and *function* (pragmatics). Central Auditory Processing Disorder (CAPD) is also included here as a language disorder.

Form

Form pertains to the use, order, and sequencing of individual sounds, syllables, and words.

- Specific rules apply to form (e.g., pluralization and subject-verb number agreement). The sender and receiver need to understand and follow the rules to effectively communicate.

Phonological Disorders

Phonological disorders affect the speaker's production of phonemes, or sounds.

- Pattern errors include consistent misuse or absence of a group of sounds that have similar characteristics (e.g., voiced/unvoiced, cluster reduction).

- Errors increase as the phonological complexity of the word increases.

Morphological Disorders

A *morpheme* is the smallest meaningful unit of language.

- A morpheme may stand alone (free morpheme) or it may have to be attached to other words (bound morpheme).

    ✔ For example: *eye* = free morpheme; /s/ = bound morpheme; *eyes* has two morphemes: one free (eye) + one bound (/s/)

- Children with learning disabilities are delayed in their use of irregular verbs, prefixes, and suffixes (Paul 1995).

- Morphological omissions and errors are frequently noted in verbal and written expression.

  ✔ For example: *He ran slow.* (omission of adverb marker *-ly,* in *slowly*)

Syntactical Errors

Syntax governs the order and combination of words to form sentences ("Definitions" 1993).

- Persons with learning disabilities may not exhibit a significant number of syntactical errors in their verbal or written expression, but they may have significant difficulty *understanding* syntactically complex sentences.

  ✔ For example, in the sentence, "John, before you call your friend, go outside and ask Dad if he needs your help fixing your bike," John would probably carry out the directions in the order mentioned (i.e., first call his friend), and ignore the signal *before* as an important sequential component in the direction.

Content

Content refers to the meaning of words and sentences.

- Meaning can be assigned to an isolated, decontextualized word (e.g., *building*) or to words within context (e.g., *He is in the building*).

- Deficits may be noted in receptive and expressive language and in decontextualized and contextual situations.

- Some people also have more difficulty with one type of language task (i.e., expressive language in decontextualized situations).

Semantic Disorders

Semantics governs the meanings of words and sentences.

- People with LD have less varied vocabulary and they overuse high-frequency words such as nouns, verbs, and pronouns. They have difficulty understanding and using abstract language like similes and metaphors.

Function

Function is how language is used.

- Some examples of functional language are:

  ✔ storytelling

  ✔ informing

  ✔ arguing

  ✔ beginning and ending conversations

Pragmatic Disorders

Pragmatics is the system that combines form and content of language into functionally and socially appropriate communication.

- People who are pragmatically disordered may be described as "socially inappropriate" or "have difficulty fitting in."

- They have difficulty reading their listener's need for clarification, repetition, or turn-taking during conversation, and as a result, they appear uninterested.

- Conversation may be marked by hesitations due to word-finding difficulties and use of fillers (e.g., "uh," "you know").

Central Auditory Processing Disorder (CAPD)

Central auditory processing disorders are deficits in processing audible signals, and these deficits are not the result of a hearing loss. Many individuals with learning disabilities have CAPD, and these difficulties are often included as one of the characteristics of a language disorder. People with CAPD have difficulty:

✔ attending, discriminating, and identifying auditory signals

✔ transforming and transmitting information through the hearing mechanism

✔ filtering, sorting, and combining information at appropriate perceptual and conceptual levels

✔ storing and retrieving information efficiently, restoring, organizing, and using retrieved information

✔ segmenting and decoding acoustic stimuli using phonological, semantic, syntactic, and pragmatic knowledge

✔ attaching meaning to connected acoustic signals through use of linguistic and nonlinguistic contexts ("Definitions" 1993)

Characteristics . . . .

Communication disorders associated with learning disabilities vary in severity and significance. As children mature, articulation errors become more noticeable and socially stigmatizing. Teachers expect students to use and understand more complex language structures. The table on page 55 lists communication characteristics often identified in children with learning disabilities.

Hearing	Speech	Language	CAPD
delayed receptive and expressive language	delayed speech development	delayed language development	doesn't retell words in sequential order
delayed speech development	limited speech production	uses nonspecific vocabulary	difficulty following directions
misarticulation of speech sounds	higher incidence of language disorders	speaks/writes in short, simple sentences	problems rhyming words
uses visual cues and strategies	difficult to understand speech in context	has word-finding difficulties	delays in learning phonics
speaks in a loud or soft volume	voice disorders are frequently present	overuses verbal fillers (e.g., *uh*, *like*)	difficulty remembering sequential information
confusion understanding certain sounds	speech errors evident beyond developmental period	difficulty grasping abstract concepts of time and space	confusion with sounds and words that sound similar (e.g., *b/p*, *soccer/sucker*)
speech and language contains less diverse vocabulary	prevalent sound substitution errors (e.g., *w/r* as in *rabbit*)	difficulty comprehending spoken and written information	forgets daily routines
speech and language have less complex syntax	difficulty eliciting correct production of speech errors	difficulty generalizing rules and learning strategies	doesn't easily recognize visual and auditory word patterns (e.g., VC-closed syllable)
difficulty relating to peers	interacts inappropriately with peers	difficulty understanding and using rules to form words (e.g., root words + affixes)	inappropriate answers to *wh-* questions
	reluctant to participate in oral discussions	spelling error patterns may be consistent with reading and speech errors	inattentive, daydreams
		confusion with articles (*a, an, the*) and conjunctions (*but, so, because*)	disorganized and "forgetful"

Screening ....

The purpose of screening for communication disorders is to identify a possible hearing, speech, or language disorder. School systems routinely screen students' hearing and communication skills, but teachers, parents, and spouses may observe or report behaviors that indicate a communication disorder.

The checklist on page 57 may help identify the presence of a communication disorder. Check the column that indicates the behavior's frequency. The behaviors can be directly observed or reported, and the information can be shared with a speech-language pathologist who may recommend additional testing.

Communication Screening Checklist

Name_____

Seldom = S   Frequently = F   Always = A

Skills	S	F	A
Hearing			
speaks in an inappropriate loud or soft voice			
listens to loud music or turns up TV volume			
difficulty understanding conversation in a noisy environment			
omits word endings in spoken or written language			
has ear infections			
Speech			
mispronounces sounds in words			
speech is difficult to understand			
mispronunciations are consistent			
hesitates and repeats sounds and syllables			
tension and struggle accompany hesitations and repetitions of speech sounds			
voice sounds "harsh," "breathy," or "hoarse"			
speaking volume or pitch is not typical of peers' voices			
Language			
uses nonspecific vocabulary			
length and complexity of sentences are limited			
grammatical errors in speech and written work			
difficulty following oral and/or written directions			
difficulty understanding oral discussions or reading passages			
difficulty initiating and maintaining a conversation			
Central Auditory Processing			
appears to "daydream"			
difficulty with phonics skills			
difficulty remembering orally-presented information and directions			
difficulty repeating sequential information			
pauses for an inappropriate length of time before responding			
repetition is required for understanding			
frequently confuses similar-sounding words			

Intervention . . . .

Speech-language pathologists are primarily responsible for the evaluation and treatment of communication disorders. Teachers, parents, and related professionals should work together to develop a specific intervention plan. You can use these strategies to supplement an existing treatment plan or to foster communication skills.

Hearing

Intervention depends primarily on the type and severity of the hearing loss. Sensori-neural hearing loss frequently requires amplification or a hearing aid. A person with a congenital hearing loss may need auditory training and aural rehabilitation techniques. Children with a moderate to severe hearing loss may need special education placement.

When talking to someone who has a sensori-neural hearing loss:

✔ get the listener's attention before speaking to him/her

✔ face the person when speaking

✔ speak in a "normal" voice (i.e., not too slowly or loudly)

✔ provide visual cues prior to and during instruction

✔ ask the listener to give feedback about oral discussions to check comprehension

✔ eliminate or reduce any distracting noise in the listening environment

✔ give the person preferred seating (e.g., close to the person giving instruction and away from glare of the blackboard)

A temporary conductive hearing loss may need short-term medical attention, while permanent conductive hearing losses may need ongoing medical follow-up. In addition to medical intervention, an assistive listening device or amplification may be needed for a permanent conductive hearing loss. The physician, audiologist, and SLP should lead the team in developing an appropriate intervention plan. Many suggestions for a sensori-neural hearing loss will also work for conductive hearing losses.

Hearing Loss Strategies

S   =   State the topic to be discussed.

P   =   Pace your conversation using appropriate rate and volume.

E   =   Enunciate clearly.

E   =   Engage in conversation using natural gestures.

CH   =   Check comprehension before changing topics.

Adapted from L.J. Hood (1998)

Speech

The SLP is responsible for designing and implementing specific intervention strategies, but other professionals and parents can implement some intervention strategies. The following strategies are appropriate to all three areas of speech.

General Speech Techniques

- Provide a "good" speech model when talking or reading aloud.

- Speak at a normal rate and volume of speech.

- Be a patient listener, allow the speaker to finish talking, and don't interrupt or finish the sentence for him/her.

- Provide multiple opportunities for the person to speak in a stress-free environment.

Language

Use the following language intervention techniques as goals regardless of the technique you choose.

Language Intervention Techniques

- Infuse instruction into daily routines and activities to increase generalization of language skills in a variety of settings.

- Use materials in the intervention plan that are familiar and commonly found in the environment.

- Provide numerous opportunities for the person to "practice" language skills with different speakers and listeners.

- Include all aspects of language (form, function, use) into each intervention/activity; language competency cannot be developed by teaching discrete, isolated skills.

- Place language intervention activities within meaningful contexts and in realistic situations.

Intervention Strategies . . . .

Joint-Action Activities

Joint-action routines involve two people and typically focus on a familiar, predictable activity (Roth and Worthington 1996). The activity includes a sequence of events that foster verbal interaction with multiple opportunities to develop and practice pragmatic language skills, such as turn-taking. Play-based activities (e.g., role playing, board games) provide stress-free contexts for language intervention.

In the example below, the teacher (Ms. Smith) plays Principal Jones, and the student (Michael) plays the messenger. Both roles are typical of the environment.

Activity: role playing and relaying information

Language Target: greetings, informing, clarifying, closings

Setting: school office

Michael/Messenger:	(to secretary) Hello. My teacher, Ms. Smith, wants me to give Ms. Jones a message about the field trip our class is taking on Friday.
Ms. Smith/Principal Jones:	Hi. What can I do for you?
Michael/Messenger:	Hi. Ms. Smith wants me to tell you that we have 28 students going on the field trip Friday.
Ms. Smith/Principal Jones:	That's fine. How many parents are going with your class?
Michael/Messenger:	I don't know.

At this point in the dialogue, Ms. Smith/Principal Jones provides Michael/Messenger with strategies to expand his message and develop his pragmatic language skills.

Ms. Smith/Principal Jones:	It's important for me to know how many parents will be going. (expectant pause)
Michael/Messenger:	I can ask Ms. Smith and come back and tell you, or she could call you on the intercom.
Ms. Smith/Principal Jones:	Great idea! I would like you to go back to Ms. Smith and ask her how many parents will be going with your class on the field trip. Then she can call the office on the intercom and give me the information. Okay?
Michael/Messenger:	Okay. Bye.

Ms. Smith again provides Michael with a model that expands his closing, and this helps develop his pragmatic language skills within a naturally-occurring context.

> *Ms. Smith/Principal Jones*: Bye Michael. Thank you for the message.
>
> *Michael/Messenger*: Bye Ms. Jones. You're welcome.

Daily Routines

Daily routines such as circle time and peer-group work provide opportunities for repeated practice of language skills within a meaningful context. Try to target specific skills like appropriate greetings, concepts, and vocabulary within a regularly-occurring routine. Here are some steps you can take:

1. Examine the setting and identify routines that occur on a daily basis or that follow a repeated format and sequence of events. Choose a routine that the person enjoys.

2. Identify the language skill that will be targeted during the routine.

3. Provide a direct model of the targeted language behavior.

> **Activity:** morning circle time
>
> **Language Target:** social greetings and responses, topic maintenance
>
> *Teacher*: Good morning. It's cold this morning. I had to find my heavy coat and gloves before I could go outside. Lara, how are you this cold morning?
>
> *Lara*: I'm cold, too. (or) I'm fine. (Lara's language target should be an appropriate social response to the teacher's greeting. Lara should continue the conversational topic about coldness. For example, I wore my heavy coat today. [or] I couldn't find my gloves this morning.)

In the example above, the teacher provides an appropriate model for social greetings and responses, and a topical, familiar conversational opener. Various aspects of language (e.g., pragmatics, semantics) were also simultaneously targeted during the routine.

Activity-Based Intervention

Activity-based intervention has activities that generally do *not* occur regularly (e.g., field trips, art activities, and baking projects). Specific language targets are often identified prior to the activity, but additional targets may be included as the activity unfolds.

Activity: baking brownies

Language Target: following sequential, multi-part instructions

Teacher: Now, we have all of our ingredients. Let's read and follow the directions on the back of the box. First we need to measure ¾ cup of water. Jaime, would you do that for us, please?

Jaime: I don't know how to do that.

The teacher realizes that Jaime doesn't appear to understand the concept of fractions, so he can't functionally apply that information. The teacher expands Jaime's language target to include the concept of fractions and their functional application.

Revised Language Target:
1. following sequential, multi-part instructions
2. understanding fractions
3. applying knowledge of fractions

Central Auditory Processing Disorders (CAPD)

To process auditory information, you must identify, discriminate, store, retrieve, analyze, and synthesize sounds such as environmental, speech, and spoken-word sounds to process auditory information. Persons with CAPD rely heavily on contextual cues to help them decode auditory information. Use a multisensory approach that incorporates materials like textbooks, vocabulary word lists, and spelling words into the intervention plan and provides meaningful contexts.

Activity: spelling lesson on short vowel and long vowel words

Language Target: to discriminate vowel sounds in words

Teacher: I'm going to say two words from this week's spelling lesson. I want you to listen and to tell me if the two words sound the same or different. Let's start with Sharyn. Here are two words: *slap   sleep*. Sharyn, do these two words sound the same or different?

In the previous example, the teacher uses the weekly spelling words to help Sharyn improve her auditory discrimination skills. This activity is realistic, occurs frequently in the classroom, and the opportunity for generalization increases because Sharyn uses the words in a variety of activities. You can also use the same weekly spelling words to target other auditory processing skills such as:

- **sound analysis** (Which word has the long vowel sound, *slap* or *sleep*?)

- **closure** (Complete the word by filling in the missing sound using a short vowel or long vowel; *sl_____ p*.)

- **blending** (Blend the sounds to complete the word, sl --- a --- p; sl --- ee --- p.)

Summary . . . .

Communication disorders occur frequently in children and adults. Hearing disorders may be temporary or permanent conditions that require medical attention and/or amplification. Speech disorders include problems with articulation, voice, or fluency. Articulation disorders are the most common speech disorders, and stuttering is the most recognized.

Language disorders are prevalent in school-aged children and contribute directly to academic difficulties. Delays in reading development and dyslexia can often be attributed to auditory processing deficits. People with learning disabilities have deficits in receptive and expressive language. Phonological disorders exist beyond the developmental language period, and limitations in morphology, semantics, and pragmatics are often identified in adults with learning disabilities. The speech-language pathologist and audiologist are primarily responsible for assessing and treating persons with communication disorders, but general intervention goals and strategies can be incorporated into the preschool and academic curriculum.

■ ■

References and Resources . . . .

Castrogiovanni, A., "Incidence and Prevalence of Speech, Voice, and Language Disorders in the United States," *Communication Facts 2000 Edition*, American Speech-Language-Hearing Association, Rockville, MD, 2000.

Daly, D. A., *The Source for Stuttering and Cluttering*, LinguiSystems, East Moline, IL, 1996.

"Definitions of Communication Disorders and Variations," *American Speech-Language-Hearing Association*, Vol. 35, Suppl. 10, 1993, pp. 40-41.

"Diagnostic and Statistical Manual for Mental Disorders, 4th Ed.," (DSM-IV), American Psychiatric Association, Washington, D.C., 1994.

Hood, L. J., "Short- and Long-Term Effects of Otitis Media on Hearing," Paper presented at annual meeting of the Speech Pathologists & Audiologists in Louisiana Schools, Alexandria, LA, September, 1998.

Kuder, S. J., *Teaching Students with Language and Communication Disabilities*, Allyn & Bacon, Boston, 1997.

LDonline, n.d., <http://www.ldonline.org/abcs_info/ld_types.html> (March 18, 1999).

Paul, R., *Language Disorders from Infancy through Adolescence: Assessment & Intervention*, Mosby, St. Louis, MO, 1995.

Roth, F. P. and Worthington, C. K., *Treatment Resource Manual for Speech-Language Pathology*, Singular, San Diego, 1996.

. . . .

Alexander Graham Bell Association for the Deaf
3417 Volta Place, NW
Washington, D.C. 20007-2778
202-337-5220
<http://www.agbell.org>

American Speech-Language-Hearing Association (ASHA)
10801 Rockville Pike
Rockville, MD 20852
301-897-5700

Children and Adults with Attention Deficit Disorder (CHADD)
8181 Professional Place, Suite 201
Landover, MD 20785
301-306-7070
<www. chadd.org>

KidSource OnLine
<www.kidsource.com>

Learning Disabilities Association of America (LDA)
4156 Library Road
Pittsburgh, PA 15234-1379
412-341-1515
<www.ldanatl.org>

National Center for Learning Disabilities
<www.ncld.org/ld/info_ld2.html>
<www.ncld.org/brochures/geninfo.html>

National Council on Stuttering
9242 Gross Point Road, #305
Skokie, IL 60077-1338
708-677-8280

National Stuttering Project
5100 E. LaPalma Avenue, Suite 208
Anaheim Hills, CA 92807
800-364-1677 or 714-693-7480
<www.nspstutter.org>

Stuttering Foundation of America
3100 Walnut Grove Road, Suite 603
P.O. Box 11749
Memphis, TN   38111-0749
800-992-9392
<www.stuttersfa.org>

National Center for Learning Disabilities
381 Park Avenue South, Suite 1401
New York, NY 10016

■ ■

Dyslexia

It's the first day of the school year and Carl, a sixth grader, is dreading getting up. A happy, confident child during the summer months, Carl is sullen as he dresses for the first day of school. Except for Bs in math and art, Carl got all Ds on his last report card. He especially struggled in reading. He dreads reading aloud because he often mispronounces even simple words. When the teacher asks about the reading assignment, Carl usually doesn't know the answers. If he does, he has a hard time quickly putting the answers into words when called on. He also hates going outside of class with the resource teacher for science and social studies. He knows a lot about science and social studies. If only the textbooks were easier to read!

Carl's experience with reading is not uncommon—it's typical of students with dyslexia. As students progress through school, they need better reading skills each year to understand textbooks and do well in subject areas. If they don't develop these skills, they get further and further behind. Self-esteem falls, and an academic crisis develops.

Definition

According to the International Dyslexia Society (IDA), people with dyslexia have difficulties translating language into thought, and thought into language ("Definition" 1994). Dyslexia is characterized by problems with expressive and receptive language that are usually related to inadequate phonological processing. This causes difficulties in reading, writing, spelling, handwriting, and sometimes, mathematics.

Dyslexia is a problem with *language*, not intelligence (Jordan 1996). In fact, many experts limit a diagnosis of dyslexia to students with IQ scores over 80 (Spafford and Grosser 1996). As with many other learning disabilities, unexpected underachievement is a classic characteristic. People never outgrow dyslexia, but they can learn to cope and to succeed in school and life with appropriate interventions.

The term *dyslexia* is sometimes inappropriately used to describe any type of reading difficulty, but not everyone who has a reading problem has dyslexia. Some people who read poorly have garden-variety reading problems due to factors such as inadequate instruction, below average intelligence, or poor motivation. Reading problems may also be associated with visual or hearing impairments, attention deficit disorder, general developmental disability, or other conditions (Snow, et. al. 1998). These factors may coexist with the dyslexia but they don't cause it.

Dyslexia is inherited, runs in families, and is thought to be caused by brain and chromosome differences (Jordan 1996; Lyon, "Research" 1995; Pennington 1991). People with dyslexia often have remarkable talents and excel in art, science, and technical fields. Some famous people thought to have been dyslexic include Albert Einstein, Winston Churchill, Hans Christian Anderson, Woodrow Wilson, Leonardo da Vinci, Thomas Edison, George Patton, William Butler Yeats, Nelson Rockefeller, Bruce Jenner, and Tom Cruise (Pennington 1991; West 1997).

Incidence

Many researchers have different definitions for dyslexia, and people with learning disabilities often have overlapping conditions. As a result, there is much confusion regarding the incidence of dyslexia.

Spafford and Grosser estimate that at least 2-5% of the U.S. population has dyslexia (1996). However, other researchers think the percentage could run as high as 15% (Richardson 1994). According to Lyon, about 10 million children or around 17% have reading difficulties. Approximately 80-85% of children identified as learning disabled for special education services have their primary problems with reading and language (Lyon, "Keynote" 1995).

It is now believed both males and females are approximately equally at risk for dyslexia; however, girls are not identified as often as boys because boys are more likely to have behavior problems when they have trouble learning (Lyon, "Keynote" 1995; Spafford and Grosser 1996).

Characteristics of Dyslexia:

- **inadequate phonological processing**

- **inherited, runs in families**

- **cause may be related to brain and chromosomal differences**

- **incidence numbers vary: 2-15% of population**

- **males and females equally affected (but girls diagnosed less)**

Characteristics ·

No two people with dyslexia are alike. Some may have many symptoms while others may have only a few. Most have strengths that can disguise the dyslexia or call attention away from it. For example, very intelligent children with dyslexia often use their background experiences and listening skills to understand written text without reading it adequately. At some point these concepts and skills become so difficult that coping skills break down and the student begins to fail. This usually happens around third or fourth grade when children start to read textbooks independently to learn. Some students make it to high school or college before becoming overwhelmed with reading difficulties. Many suffer problems of low self-esteem due to the disability.

Identification of dyslexia is difficult because characteristics may be so different. Symptoms can range from very mild to profound. See the chart *Characteristics of Dyslexia* on page 69 for major characteristics and some examples of behavior. Keep in mind these characteristics are detrimental only after they are no longer age-appropriate. For example, one would not expect a two-year old to have good phonemic awareness, handwriting is usually difficult for a four-year old, and many kindergarten and first graders have problems with directionality in mathematics.

Characteristics of Dyslexia

lack of phonological awareness
delayed spoken language
poor sequencing of letters or numbers (*aminal* for *animal*, *bakset* for *basket*, *gril* for *girl*)
confusion about directionality in space or time (*left* and *right*; *up* and *down*; *before* and *after*; *m*, *w*, and *3*; *n* and *u*; *7* and *L*; *21* and *12*)
difficulty decoding (sounding out words)
difficulty encoding (spelling)
reading comprehension problems
problems with written expression (organizing and expressing ideas)
handwriting difficulties
central auditory processing problems (poor interpretation of what is heard)
oral expression difficulties
right- or left-handedness confusion
problems in mathematics related to sequencing, directionality, or mathematical language
International Dyslexia Association, 1996

Screening . . . .

Identify students as at-risk for dyslexia *before* they fail. Use the checklist on page 71 as one screening tool. Check the column that indicates the frequency of the directly observed or reported behavior. Tally the number and frequency that the behaviors occur. Also use other diverse sources to make a good diagnosis: work samples; interviews; questionnaires completed by teachers and family members; observations; informal writing samples; self-assessments; test scores; and medical, familial, and educational histories.

If this checklist indicates that a student may have dyslexia, more intense, in-depth assessment by a team of professionals is needed. Keep in mind that these characteristics indicate the possibility of dyslexia only if they are not appropriate for the student's age and educational background.

Dyslexia Screening Checklist

Name_____

Seldom = S   Frequently = F   Always = A

Characteristic	S	F	A
poor phonemic awareness (awareness of sounds within words, rhyming, segmenting or manipulating sounds)			
poor phonological processing			
delayed spoken language			
difficulty decoding words (especially if trying to use phonics)			
lack of fluency or automaticity when reading orally (e.g., mispronouncing words, skipping lines, rereading lines, running words together, or leaving them out)			
adding or deleting letters, sounds, or syllables from words			
poor reading comprehension			
subvocalizing/finger tracking print when reading, subvocalizing when writing			
very poor spelling abilities			
misshapen or laborious handwriting			
poor written composition			
problems recalling names of events, people, places, names of objects, etc.			
difficulty sequencing alphabet, numbers, days of week, months of year, etc.			
scrambling or reversing letters, words, and/or numbers			
problems with directionality (e.g., *before/after*, *right/left*, *top/bottom*)			
confusion with prepositions and articles (e.g., *in/on/at*, *with/about*, *a/an*)			
unclear hand preference			
difficulty expressing ideas orally, especially if not prepared beforehand			
delay in verbal response			
difficulty comprehending what is heard (e.g., has problems following oral directions, needs information repeated, frequently misunderstands)			
very literal interpretation of slang or figurative language			
more of a literal than an abstract thinker			
poor copying skills at near- or far-point			
problems with time or space			
disorganization			
extreme difficulty learning a foreign language			
problems with math related to language, sequencing, or directionality			
poor performance on tests (especially timed tests)			
very slow at completing tasks involving reading and/or writing			
performance inconsistencies (e.g., knows material one day only to forget it the next, can perform a complex task but not a related simple one)			
extreme frustration, anxiety, and avoidance when faced with language tasks			
achievement incommensurate with intellectual ability			
family history of similar problems			

Intervention . . . .

The International Dyslexia Association (Schupack and Wilson 1997) recommends specific criteria for instruction for students with dyslexia:

Criteria for Instruction

1. Diagnostic Teaching

Students' strengths and weaknesses will vary. Assessment should be ongoing during instruction, and instruction should be individualized. Students learn best in one-on-one or small group situations. Begin at the student's level and be flexible in planning and teaching. Pacing should be appropriate—not too fast or too slow. Provide materials on appropriate reading levels.

2. Multisensory Instruction

People with dyslexia learn differently so they need multisensory instruction that simultaneously sends information to the brain along multiple pathways (visual, auditory, tactile, kinesthetic).

3. Systematic, Cumulative Language Concepts

Language instruction should start with the simplest concepts and move to more complex ones in an orderly way. One concept should build on the other.

4. Explicit, Direct Instruction

People with dyslexia do not pick up language concepts easily or through incidental learning. They need direct instruction with specific rules, examples, and applications to real life. Provide frequent teacher-student interaction with opportunities for active learning and systematic review.

5. Synthetic and Analytic Instruction

Students often benefit from part-to-whole instruction (synthetic) within meaningful contexts. Break learning down to its smallest parts and teach each part. Students also need whole-to-part instruction (analytic) to break down unfamiliar words in context, extract details from stories, etc. Do both types of instruction in a consistent, risk-free learning environment.

6. Phonology/Phonological Awareness

Examples of appropriate phonology and phonological awareness activities include rhyming games, identifying words that sound similar or different, isolating sounds in words, changing the beginning or endings of words, and clapping word segments. Most students with dyslexia need to continue to work on phonemic awareness activities even after peers are proficient.

7. Graphophonemic Relationships

Teach graphophonemic (sound-symbol) relationships with visual-to-auditory and auditory-to-visual clues. Students need to build a vocabulary base of phonetically-regular words before working with irregular words.

8. Morphology/Syllabication

Morphology (meaningful word parts) includes root word, affixes, compound words, contractions, etc. Morphology helps students with dyslexia understand written and spoken language. Help students learn about basic word parts and use this knowledge to decode and comprehend.

9. Syntax

Students with dyslexia do not always pick up syntax (word order and function in sentences) intuitively. Provide instruction and experiences with simple and complex sentence patterns.

10. Semantics

Students with dyslexia should analyze and study words with multiple meanings, opposite meanings, similar meanings, etc. Teach comprehension strategies to understand narrative and expository text.

Intervention Strategies . . . .

People with dyslexia can learn successfully if they use strategies to either master concepts and skills or compensate for weaknesses. The strategies in this section are not all-inclusive. They should serve as a springboard to help teachers analyze students' needs and ways to meet them. There are five main categories: General Considerations, Organization, Classroom Instruction, Language Arts, and Test Taking.

General Considerations

Before beginning specific interventions, consider the following strategies:

Encourage Students to Get Extra Help from Tutors

- Make sure effective tutors:
  - ✔ understand the characteristics of dyslexia
  - ✔ have a sound educational background
  - ✔ know multisensory techniques
  - ✔ establish good rapport with student
  - ✔ build student's self-esteem
  - ✔ set appropriate goals

Make Instruction Meaningful

- Provide all instruction in authentic, purposeful contexts. These contexts can include:
  - ✔ original stories or poems
  - ✔ notes to parents
  - ✔ menus of familiar restaurants
  - ✔ street signs
  - ✔ letters to and from friends
  - ✔ computer and video game manuals
  - ✔ popular books and short stories
  - ✔ cookbook recipes

- Integrate reading, writing, speaking, and listening activities in school, just as they are integrated in real life.

- Encourage students to enjoy reading and writing. The more they read and write, the better readers and writers they will become.

Help Students Find Areas of Excellence

- Help students find talents in sports, drama, art, and music.

- Encourage them to find jobs at which they might do well (baby-sitting, camp counseling, pet sitting).

- Help students appreciate each other's strengths.

- Never take away an area of excellence as punishment for poor grades due to dyslexia.

Organization

Organization is an important step in helping students with dyslexia. Using a calendar, following a routine, and color-coding books are some of the strategies discussed in this section.

Keep a Calendar

- Since external organization is sometimes a problem for students with dyslexia, teach them to keep a calendar with due dates for assignments and extracurricular activities.

- Help students break assignments down into the smallest parts and assign due dates for each part.

- Have students confer with their teacher (parent, tutor) after each part is completed.

Set a Routine

- Help students maintain a consistent homework routine, find a special place to do homework, and determine a way to organize supplies.

- Allow students frequent breaks and plenty of time.

- To decide on a routine, have students ask themselves:

  - ✔ What time do I need to start?

  - ✔ How much time should I allow to finish?

  - ✔ What other activities do I have to do?

  - ✔ Will I need help and where can I get it?

Choose Textbooks Carefully

- Provide well-organized textbooks that have bold headings and easy-to-understand charts and diagrams.

- If possible, provide one set of books for the student to keep at school and another set at home.

- Help students color-code books and notebooks (e.g, red for English, green for math) and keep an assignment book in which to write and check off daily assignments.

- Allow students to highlight and write in books, if possible. If not, encourage them to use sticky notes to mark passages or pages.

Classroom Instruction

Strategies for classroom instruction include ways to structure lessons, time issues, and multisensory learning.

Structure and Organize Instruction

- Organize classroom lessons well.

- State and write the lesson objectives on an overhead projector or board before beginning class. Give students an outline or a study sheet to guide them as they listen and before they take notes.

- If poor note-taking interferes with learning, provide a copy of the notes and overhead transparencies, or a peer can share notes with the struggling classmate.

The Source for Learning Disabilities
Copyright © 2000 LinguiSystems, Inc.

- Allow students with dyslexia to audiotape class activities.

- Provide frequent, short review sessions rather than one long session right before testing.

- Use various methods of instruction such as lectures with visual aids, cooperative groups, games, computer projects, simulations, movement activities, and hands-on activities.

Post Directions and Sequencing Aides

- State, post, and paraphrase directions using concrete examples. Students can then paraphrase the directions themselves and begin work under teacher supervision to make sure they understand. Later they can refer to what has been posted or listen to the directions on tape.

- Post the alphabet, number line, calendar, daily schedule, and other sequencing aides either on the wall or at students' desks. Also post sequenced, step-by-step instructions for projects and study methods.

Provide Sample Projects for Models

- Call attention to the sequence and organization of the sample items and allow students to examine them.

Keep Time in Mind

- When reading and writing are involved, you may need to assign shorter assignments with more time to do them, and let students know about the assignment in advance.

- Allow students to wait before responding to oral questions.   You may need to advise some students of oral questions or readings ahead of time so they can practice.

- Allow oral reports or other performance-based projects to demonstrate learning rather than writing reports.

- Reduce some assignments to only the essentials required for mastery.

- Provide frequent rest breaks, praise, and encouragement.

- Teachers and students should agree on any special conditions at the beginning of a task rather than haphazardly adding them later.

Make Study Multisensory

- When studying new material, the teacher, tutor, or student can highlight the most important information in the text. Then the student (or teacher or tutor) can read it into a tape recorder. Students can later write important terms, definitions, and other data on a rough surface with two fingers (e.g., sandpaper, a salt tray, carpet square, blue jeans leg) while they listen to the tape and say the information simultaneously. This allows them to use auditory, visual, tactile, and kinesthetic channels.

- Have students quickly write their thoughts down as they say them aloud if this works better for them.

- Encourage students with dyslexia to study with a partner or a group so that more senses are involved. Have students act out a story, science experiment, or historical scene. Put ideas to music or dance or use mnemonic devices to help these students remember.

- Multisensory study is usually slower and more tiring than more traditional methods, and over-learning is often necessary. Give students more time to study.

- Ask the students to suggest multisensory methods that they think will help them. Parents and educators often forget to do this. Self-understanding and self-assessment are important components for students with dyslexia.

Language Arts

Language Arts is the primary area of concern for students with dyslexia. Strategies for reading, listening, and speaking are in this section. Strategies for spelling and writing are found in Chapter 5, Dysgraphia.

Reading

Poor reading abilities characterize students with dyslexia. The following strategies will help students with decoding and comprehension.

Supply Materials at the Appropriate Reading Level

- Ask librarians and colleagues with experience in lower grades for help finding easier versions of stories or content area texts.

- Choose books with pictures that are not considered "babyish" by students. Many companies now publish high interest/low ability level books to motivate students.

- Rewrite selections in simple words or provide summaries of text.

- Search bookstores for abbreviated versions of literature.

Convey the Purpose

- Students need to know why they are reading. Explain purposes through discussion or by providing a few basic questions before you begin.

- Activate students' prior knowledge about reading topics with discussion, pictures, and concrete experiences before beginning to read.

Practice Tracking

- Teach students with dyslexia how to track print as they read with a finger, pencil, strip of paper, or window card (a small card with a hole the size of a word or line cut in the center).

- Have students try putting checkmarks by lines as they finish them.

- As they track, allow students to subvocalize (move their lips to read inaudibly or softly to themselves) to fully comprehend a passage.

Use Word Attack

- Teach word-attack skills. Give special emphasis to phonemic awareness and graphophonics, but help students become proficient with context clues, syntax, structural analysis, sight words, word origins, word meanings, etc. Students need a lot of multisensory practice with these skills so decoding will become automatic and not interrupt the flow of meaning.

Be Conscious of Problem Words

- People with dyslexia usually have difficulty reading words with similar spellings (*from/for/form, on/no, tab/tap*) and function words (*who, when, where*). Have students write these words with raised letters on cards so they can trace, say, and look at them at the same time. Post the words with clues next to them if necessary.

Teach Students to Self-Monitor Reading

- Students with dyslexia often concentrate so hard on decoding words that they don't realize they're not understanding the meaning. Teach them to self-monitor their reading and have them ask questions like:

   ✔ Am I understanding what I am reading?

   ✔ If not, what can I do to understand? Reread? Ask the meaning of a word? Stop to discuss with a friend?

Use Follow-Up Activities

- Assign follow-up activities after reading that focus on comprehension and skill development. Provide ample time for questions, discussion, and multisensory activities.

- Have students read orally for real purposes (e.g., to prove an answer to a question, to demonstrate a character's emotions, or to act out a story). Carefully monitor areas like pronunciation and fluency.

- Read interesting stories more than once to help students develop fluency, automaticity, and confidence.

Read Aloud to Students

- Read stories aloud to let students experience good literature and rich vocabulary above their own reading levels. If they have their own copies of these selections, they can read along with you. Visualization, drama, and art projects help stories come alive.

- Provide audio-taped texts. Have students read orally as they follow along. Volunteers, parents, or tutors can tape textbooks. Students can also join *Recording for the Blind & Dyslexic*, a private, nonprofit organization that provides taped texts. (See references on page 85).

The Source for Learning Disabilities
Copyright © 2000 LinguiSystems, Inc.

Listening & Speaking

Although listening and speaking are strong points for some students with dyslexia, others need direct, multisensory instruction. You might need to teach skills like:

✔ expressing oneself effectively

✔ entering and exiting informal conversations

✔ giving formal speeches

✔ listening actively

✔ understanding viewpoints of other speakers

Practice Practice Practice

• Students need many opportunities to practice speaking and listening. Develop stress-free, authentic situations such as peer discussions, teacher-student conferences, book reports, written composition sharing and responding, class newspaper interviews, and storytellings.

Make Activities Short and Clear

• Short, meaningful assignments are much better than long, tedious ones.

• Give students immediate and constructive feedback.

• Teach listening using cloze procedures in which students finish partially-completed listening guides while listening to class lectures, discussions, videos, etc.

• When planning oral speeches, provide explicit frameworks and goals for students to follow.

• As listening and speaking improve, modify frameworks and guides to include only basic headings that can later be withdrawn completely.

Test-Taking

Students with dyslexia often fail tests because they do not read or write well enough to pass, not because they don't know the information. Here are some strategies so you can ensure that students do their best on tests.

Make Tests Easy to Read

- Format tests appropriately and make accommodations when necessary. Tests should have large print and good spacing, and be easy to read. Test questions should be grouped according to type (e.g, multiple choice, matching, listing, essay) and go from simple to complex items. Long test sections should be avoided if possible. If matching questions are used, all premises and responses should be on the same page to reduce page turning and reading problems.

- Help students underline key words/phrases such as *circle*, *mark two responses*, and *give an example*. Have them paraphrase directions and work an item or two under your supervision to make sure they understand. Some students may need to audiotape the directions for later listening.

Prepare for Scantron Tests

- Make sure students have plenty of sharp pencils and good erasers before taking scantron tests (bubble sheets).

- Practice filling in circles or making other appropriate marks with the students before the test.

- Have students check the item number and match it to the correct line on the answer sheet for each item if necessary. Allow students to use a ruler or a card to make sure they stay on the correct line.

- Monitor students frequently to make sure they are not skipping lines or marking two answers on the same line. If answer sheets are extremely difficult to use, allow students to write directly on the test.

Make Accommodations

- If a student needs to have a test read aloud, make sure the test reader reads *exactly* what is on the test and doesn't give any clues.

- Allow some students to give their answers orally as someone else records them. The recorder should give no clues and should record answers exactly as the student gives them.

- Provide a special time and/or place to give the test.

- Audiotape the test and/or the student's responses if appropriate.

- If students write out test answers themselves, don't penalize them for spelling and language mechanics problems in content area subjects.

Discourage Test Anxiety

- Students with dyslexia may need extra time to take tests or may need to have tests broken up into more than one session. You may have to shorten tests in some cases.

- Give tests in a stress-free environment. Just knowing that extra time or an extra break will be allowed alleviates anxiety for many students.

Summary . . . .

Dyslexia is a language processing disability that is genetic and runs in families. People with dyslexia have trouble translating language into thought and thought into language. They learn differently and many are very talented. No two people with dyslexia are alike. Some may have many characteristics and others may have only a few. Characteristics range from very mild to severe.

Due to the diversity of characteristics, early identification and intervention is extremely important. People with dyslexia need explicit, systematic, multisensory instruction in language concepts. They also benefit from intervention strategies to help them compensate. Although they will never outgrow dyslexia, they can learn to cope and succeed in school and life.

. . . .

References and Resources . . . .

"Definition of Dyslexia," General Membership Meeting of the International Dyslexia Association Annual Conference, Los Angeles, CA, 1994.

"Finding the Answers," International Dyslexia Association, Baltimore, 1996.

Galaburda, A. M., "Developmental Dyslexia: A Review of Biological Interactions," *Annals of Dyslexia*, Vol. 35, 1985, pp. 21-34.

Galaburda, A. M., Rosen, G. F., and Sherman, G. D., "The Neural Origin of Developmental Dyslexia: Implications for Medicine, Neurology and Cognition," *Reading to Neurons*, MIT Press, Cambridge, MA, 1989.

Jordan, D., *Overcoming Dyslexia in Children, Adolescents, and Adults*, Pro-Ed, Austin, TX, 1996.

Knight, J., "Adults with Dyslexia: Aspiring and Achieving," International Dyslexia Association, Baltimore, 1997.

Lyon, G. R., "Keynote address," Conference of the New Jersey Branch of the Orton Dyslexia Society, New Jersey, 1995.

Lyon, G. R., "Research in Learning Disabilities: Contributions from Scientists Supported by the National Institute of Child Health and Human Development," *Journal of Child Neurology*, Vol. 10, 1995, pp. 120-126.

Pennington, B. F., *Diagnosing Learning Disorders: A Neurological Framework*, Guilford Press, New York, 1991.

Richardson, S., "Doctors Ask Questions About Dyslexia: A Review of Medical Research," International Dyslexia Association, Baltimore, 1994.

Schupack, H. and Wilson, B., "Reading, Writing, and Spelling: The Multisensory Structured Language Approach," International Dyslexia Association, Baltimore, MD, 1997.

Snow, C., Burns, M., and Griffin, P. (Eds.), *Preventing Reading Difficulties in Young Children*, National Academy Press, Washington, D.C., 1998.

Spafford, C. and Grosser, G., *Dyslexia: Research and Resource Guide*, Allyn and Bacon, Boston, MA, 1996.

Torgesen, J., "Phonological Awareness: A Critical Factor in Dyslexia," International Dyslexia Association, Baltimore, 1995.

West, T., *In the Mind's Eye*, Prometheus Books, Buffalo, NY, 1997.

■ ■

The International Dyslexia Association
8600 LaSalle Road
Chester Building, Suite 382
Baltimore, MD 21286-2044
410-296-0232 or 800-222-3123
<www.interdys.org>

LD Online
<www.ldonline.org>

Learning Disability Association
4156 Library Road
Pittsburgh, PA 15234
412-341-1515
<www.ldanatl.org>

Council for Exceptional Children
1920 Association Dr.
Reston, VA 20191-1589
1-888-CEC-SPED
<www.cec.sped.org>

Recording for the Blind & Dyslexic
20 Roszel Road
Princeton, NJ 08540
609-452-0606 or 800-221-4792
<www.rfbd.org>

International Dyslexia Association's Emeritus Series
(series of monographs on specific topics related to dyslexia)
410-296-0232

Washington Educational Telecommunications Association (WETA)
P. O. 2626
Washington, D.C. 20013
703-998-3293

■ ■

5

Dysgraphia

Kim is a bright, energetic fourteen-year-old who has just moved to a new school district. During her first week at the new school, she made the debate team and school band. She turns assignments in on time and does well if the tests are multiple choice and true/false. However, her English teacher, Mrs. Bruno, is worried because Kim's in-class assignments are illegible, unorganized, and filled with misspelled words and erasures. When Mrs. Bruno talks to Kim about the problem, Kim shrugs and says she just can't write. She tells Mrs. Bruno that her former teacher let her bring a laptop computer to class, and this helped a bit. Mrs. Bruno doesn't want to give Kim a poor grade in English because Kim will be dropped from the debate team, but she wants Kim to learn to write correctly and not rely solely on computers.

When students find it difficult to write, it affects not only their work in language arts, but content area subjects as well. Poor writing skills often limit their career choices and leisure time pursuits, also. Kim's teacher should use organized, structured, multisensory techniques and encourage Kim to use compensatory tools such as word processors, spell checkers, and laptops. Although Kim may not ever be the best writer in the class, she should be able to master basics and overcome her disability so it doesn't hamper other areas of her life.

Definition . . . .

Because the writing process is so complex, it's difficult to establish a clear definition for writing disability. Generally, a writing disability is a specific neurologically-based learning disability that affects the ability to express oneself in writing. Students' papers often have errors in spelling, punctuation, capitalization, handwriting, etc. Written compositions may also be short and unorganized with poor ideation.

Students may also have trouble executing the cognitive processes that underlie effective written expression (e.g., creating content, constructing text, planning, revising). Many people with writing disabilities have limited knowledge of the writing process and often overestimate their own writing capabilities (Graham, et. al. 1991). On the other hand, many students underestimate their capabilities and fail to achieve their potentials as writers.

Writing disabilities may or may not be accompanied by dyslexia. Some students with writing difficulties have initial problems with reading, but they respond well to reading instruction while writing continues to be a problem. Other children have writing problems without experiencing reading difficulties (Berninger 1999). Still others have both reading and writing problems that continue over time.

The term *dysgraphia* is often used when discussing writing disabilities. It can refer to extreme problems with handwriting, spelling, and written composition. It can also refer to handwriting difficulties only. We will use the first definition, and look at its subcategories of spelling, handwriting, and written composition. Someone with a writing disability may experience difficulties in one or more of these areas.

Incidence

Due to the lack of a clear-cut definition for dysgraphia and the dearth of research focused specifically on it, there are few statistics regarding prevalence. However, written language disabilities are very common in students with learning disabilities and they tend to be persistent (Berninger 1999).

Characteristics of Dysgraphia:

- **specific and neurologically-based**

- **can affect written composition, handwriting, and spelling**

- **trouble with cognitive writing process**

- **often goes hand-in-hand with dyslexia**

- **incidence numbers are difficult to determine**

Characteristics . . . .

On pages 88 and 89, you will find the typical stages of learning development for handwriting and spelling. Children with dysgraphia often have difficulty making the transitions through these stages. On page 89, you will find the components of written expression. Children with dysgraphia can lack competencies in any of these.

On page 90, you'll find a *Characteristics of Dysgraphia* chart, which lays out some of the common problems children with dysgraphia may have in handwriting, spelling, and written composition.

The Three Stages of Handwriting

Cicci 1995

1. Beginning of Graphomotor Skills or Visual Motor Integration

Children make purposeful marks with an implement (crayon, pencil, pen) on a surface (paper). They may first bump or move the implement accidentally and notice that it leaves a trace. Later they begin to make these traces deliberately until they begin scribbling. This way, they practice visual and motor skills that later lead to writing and drawing.

2. Emergence of Geometric Forms

Scribbling begins to have lines and shapes. Children imitate or copy the shapes that others draw, and these forms often represent people. Children begin to move toward a conventional pencil grasp.

3. Development of Handwriting

Children observe that marks on paper are used for communication. Squiggles take pre-letter forms. They associate meanings with the squiggles and eventually move to traditional letters.

The Five Stages of Spelling

Moats 1995

1. Precommunicative Writing

Most young children begin to experiment with writing spontaneously. At this early stage, they don't realize that letters represent speech sounds (the alphabetic principle) or that print represents words. They don't yet understand directionality and spacing. They attempt to imitate adult writing, and their writing may include letter- or number-like forms. They may assign meanings to their writing after they write but quickly forget or change the messages. When attempting to "read," they guess at whole words by looking at visual features.

2. Semiphonetic Stage

Children realize that letters represent speech sounds. A few letters (usually consonants) are used to represent entire words or syllables. Letters are usually strung together from left to right without proper spacing. Children may attempt to read using partial phonetic cues. They show awareness of the alphabetic principle when they use letters to represent speech sounds, but their spelling is crude. For example, *b* may represent *be*, *r* may represent *are*, and *kt* may represent *cat*.

3. Phonetic Stage

Children represent all phonemes in words. They know many letter names and some sound letter associations. They use invented spelling and rely heavily on sound segmentation and articulatory-phonetic feedback (movement of the mouth as they pronounce sounds). They do not show awareness of spelling patterns; for example, *nit* may represent *night*.

4. Transitional Stage

Children realize that graphemes are often groups of letters and spelling is governed by a set of patterns. They begin to use this new knowledge rather than trying to spell words exactly like they sound. Consequently, their spelling seems slightly out of sync; for example, *nite* may represent *night*.

5. Traditional Stage

Children move to traditional spelling and use rules and patterns to spell correctly.

The Three Components of Written Composition   *Hammill and Bartel 1995*

1. Cognitive Component

The cognitive component is the ability to generate written pieces that are logical, sequenced, and coherent. The piece must be understandable to the reader.

2. Linguistic Component

The linguistic component is the ability to use semantics and syntax appropriately. Use of appropriate vocabulary, sentence structure, verb tense, subject-verb agreement, etc., is necessary for good writing.

3. Stylistic Component

The stylistic component is the ability to use acceptable rules for capitalization, punctuation, and other mechanics of writing. Many of these rules are arbitrary and based on tradition, but they are often necessary to produce meaningful writing.

Characteristics of Dysgraphia

Handwriting	Spelling	Written Composition
Combination of: * • fine-motor difficulty • inability to remember motor patterns associated with letters • inability to revisualize letters	language awareness and memory problems (including letters in words)	production problems (overly simplistic; too many common words; or complex with errors in syntax, morphology, or semantics)
Types of graphomotor dysfunction: ** • motor-memory dysfunction (inability to combine motor output and memory input) • graphomotor production deficit (inability to produce graphomotor movements, awkward pencil grip, and muscle coordination) • motor feedback difficulty (trouble tracking location of pencil, face too close to the paper, use of larger muscles or joints to write)	difficulties analyzing sounds, syllables, and meaningful word parts	memory capacity deficiencies (short-term, long-term, and active working memory)
	problems learning other symbolic codes (i.e., math facts/symbols)	unsophisticated ideation (difficulty selecting a topic, brainstorming, researching, thinking critically, coming up with ideas, etc.)
	difficulty comprehending spelling rules, patterns, and structures (in older children); lack of phonemic awareness (in younger children)	organizational problems (don't know where to begin, confusion with steps)
	those with dysorthographia have orthographic memory problems (i.e., visual memory for spelling)	*Levine 1994*
* *"Just the Facts: What Is Dysgraphia?" 1998* ** *Levine 1994*	*"Just the Facts: Spelling" 1998*	

Screening

When screening for dysgraphia, take into account the number of characteristics and their severity. Use the checklist on pages 92-93 to pinpoint the exact nature of the disabilities so that appropriate instruction can be planned. Some characteristics are opposites of each other; for example, *strict phonetic spellings* and *lack of attention to phonics* are both characteristics of dysgraphia. This is because dysgraphia is complex, and symptoms for one person may be dichotomous to symptoms in another person. Check the column that indicates the frequency of the directly observed or reported behavior. Tally the number and frequency that the behaviors occur. If screening indicates the likelihood of a writing disability, a team of professionals should conduct more in-depth assessment.

Dysgraphia Screening Checklist

Name_____

Seldom = S   Frequently = F   Always = A

Handwriting	S	F	A
incorrect letter and numeral formation			
inconsistent shape and size of letters and numerals			
inconsistent slant			
tiny, cramped letter formation			
mixed uppercase and lowercase or cursive and manuscript			
confusion with directionality when writing letters or numerals (backwards, use of clockwise motions for circles, starts at bottom when should start at top, etc.)			
starts on right side of paper when writing			
poor spacing, use of margins, and positioning on lines			
difficulty staying on line when tracing			
difficulty copying simple shapes			
poor memory for letter and numeral formation			
concentrated effort to track location of pencil with eyes			
difficulty connecting cursive letters			
inefficient copying at near or far point			
awkward pencil grip			
uses large muscles in arm to move pencil			
incorrect positioning of paper			
subvocalizes when writing			
mixed-hand dominance			
poor automaticity when writing			
many erasures or cross-outs			
very poor legibility			
very slow, laborious handwriting			
very fast, scratchy handwriting			
words spelled correctly appear to be misspelled			
thoughts race ahead of ability to transcribe them			
extreme fatigue when writing by hand			
Spelling			
poor phonemic awareness			
difficulty understanding spelling rules, word structure, and/or letter patterns			
problems analyzing sounds, syllables, and word parts			
poor auditory memory for sounding out words			
poor visual memory for sequences of letters or spelling patterns			

Dysgraphia Screening Checklist, *cont.*   Name_____

Seldom = S   Frequently = F   Always = A

Spelling, *continued*	S	F	A
problems with other symbolic codes (e.g., math facts, symbols)			
strict, phonetic spellings (e.g., *fon* for *phone*)			
lack of attention to phonics when spelling (e.g., *hpoen* for *phone*)			
transposes letters (e.g., *grill* for *girl*)			
misplaces silent letters (e.g., *maek* for *make*)			
telescopes (i.e., leaves letters out, *intesting* for *interesting*)			
perseverates (i.e., adds letters, *surprisinging* for *surprising*)			
confuses word boundaries (e.g., *watoogo* for *way to go*)			
subvocalizes when spelling			
correct spelling on test but forgets very quickly			
inconsistent spelling errors (e.g., *mistak, mstaek, mistke* for *mistake*)			
lack of automaticity when spelling			
extreme fatigue when attempting to spell			
Written Composition			
difficulty choosing a topic			
inability to generate new ideas			
oversimplistic ideas			
complex ideas but cannot get them down on paper			
poor grammar, punctuation, or other mechanics			
oversimplistic sentence structure			
inability to write concise, simple, logical sentences			
inability to express complex thoughts in complex sentences			
overuse of a few common words			
chosen vocabulary words not quite right to convey intended meaning (e.g., *x-rayed* for *X-rated*)			
unable to organize writing			
loses train of thought easily when composing			
poor critical/creative thinking skills when composing			
overemphasis on neatness, etc. at expense of creativity			
extremely short, underdeveloped pieces			
writing rambles without clear beginning, middle, and end			
composition problems confounded by poor spelling			
composition problems confounded by poor handwriting			
extreme fatigue when composing			

Intervention . . . .

Poor writing abilities can negatively affect *all* academic areas. Students must receive appropriate instruction so that dysgraphia does not hinder learning in science, social studies, mathematics, and other subjects.

Instruction

Students with dysgraphia need:

1. systematic, cumulative teaching of writing concepts/skills

2. explicit, direct instruction in specific areas of weakness (i.e., handwriting, spelling, and/or composition)

3. multisensory instruction (visual, auditory, kinesthetic, tactile)

4. diagnostic teaching during which teachers continuously assess students to individualize instruction

5. instruction and practice in meaningful contexts with real purposes for writing

6. specific intervention strategies to:

✔ build on their strengths

✔ remediate/improve their weaknesses

✔ compensate for or circumvent weaknesses when remediation is not sufficient

The Source for Learning Disabilities
Copyright © 2000 LinguiSystems, Inc.

Intervention Strategies · · · · · · · · · · · · · · · · ·

People with dysgraphia can overcome their weaknesses to become better writers. Many students have found the strategies in this section helpful. Use the strategies flexibly and alter them to fit individual needs. They are divided into the three major components of handwriting, spelling, and written composition.

Handwriting

Stop Problems Early

- Stop handwriting problems early because kinesthetic memory is strong and persistent ("Just the Facts: What Is Dysgraphia?" 1999).

- Teach students to form letters correctly in kindergarten and first grade.

- Provide muscle training and over-learning of techniques.

- Teach kinesthetic writing (e.g., writing with eyes closed) to reinforce learning.

- Have students practice individual alphabet letters daily for months, if necessary.

- Teach students to say verbal cues to themselves (e.g., up, around, and down for lower case cursive *l*).

As Students Progress . . .

- The goal of instruction should be legibility and fluency, rather than perfect mastery.

- Give students alphabet charts with correctly written letters to keep at their desks. The charts can have arrows indicating directional flow so students can trace them as needed.

- Experiment with paper angles. Some students line up their letters better if they put a piece of ruled paper at a 90° angle under the writing paper so that the underlying vertical lines show through.

- Experiment with different writing tools (plastic pencil grips, mechanical pencils) and surfaces (graph paper, construction paper with lines).

- Encourage students to hold the pencil in the conventional way and allow them to practice a new grip over a period of time before expecting them to use it all of the time.

- If an unconventional grip works, don't force change.

- Encourage good posture, and provide desks and chairs that are the appropriate size.

Cursive vs. Manuscript

- Help students find writing styles that work best for them rather than insisting on a particular style.

- If students have legible manuscript handwriting but can't make the transition to cursive even with intensive effort and practice, allow them to continue using manuscript.

- Some students benefit from using cursive rather than manuscript from the beginning. Cursive eliminates the decision of where to start each letter because they all start on the line. It also helps directionality because one letter flows into the next. In addition, starting with cursive keeps students from having to make the transition from manuscript to cursive later.

- A good compromise might be *D'Nealian* which is a type of manuscript handwriting based on single-stroke pencil movements. Transition to cursive is smoother with this style (Thurber 1993).

Keyboarding and Word Processing

- Teach keyboarding and word processing early so poor handwriting doesn't interfere with other learning.

- Keep in mind that the same problems that made handwriting difficult may make keyboarding hard in the beginning.

- Capitalize on the fact that many students are motivated by computer use and can master keyboarding with time and practice.

- Provide word processors with a speech recognition program, if needed, so students can dictate their written work.

Copying

- Copying is a difficult skill for most students with dysgraphia to perform, so provide extra time and instruction.

- Determine which copying activities are really necessary and which ones can be eliminated.

- Teach copying using short, meaningful materials at near and far point.

- Before starting with a copying lesson:

    ✔ make sure students have all supplies ready

    ✔ let students know they have ample time to finish

    ✔ have students listen/look/join in as the text to be copied is read aloud and tracked several times

- Encourage students to read aloud softly as they copy.

- Have students initially copy only letters or short words, then proceed to phrases after these are mastered.

- Help students break lengthy sentences and passages down into meaningful chunks to copy.

- If poor copying interferes with learning in content area subjects:

    ✔ provide copies of boardwork and transparencies

    ✔ give copies of your class lecture notes

    ✔ allow a student's classmate to take notes using carbonless duplicating paper.

Assessment Considerations

- Make sure that poor handwriting doesn't interfere with making good grades on assessments.

- Allow students to give answers orally on tape or in person.

- Let students write directly on test papers if there are difficulties with answer sheets.

- Allow students to show learning through oral presentations and reports rather than written tests.

- Provide extended time.

Spelling

Basic Considerations

- Poor spelling permeates all curriculum areas and can be especially trying for people with dysgraphia and dyslexia ("Just the Facts: Spelling" 1998).

- Provide instruction that focuses on knowledge of:

  ✔ sounds

  ✔ letter-sound relationships

  ✔ letter-sound patterns

  ✔ syllables

  ✔ morphemes

- Focus on words that are spelled as they sound before you move to irregular words.

- Have students memorize only a few sight words at a time and have them practice the sight words often.

- Encourage students to use their spelling words in personal, meaningful ways.

- Choose spelling words that students will encounter in:

  ✔ content-area subjects

  ✔ recreational reading

  ✔ real life

Make Spelling Interesting and Fun

- Use spelling games, songs, rhymes, and drill/practice activities that use multiple senses and movement. (For example, students might write individual letters from spelling words on small slips of paper or large beans. They can then "spill" the letters for a particular word and arrange them in the right order as they say the letters and then the complete word. Afterwards, they can make a sentence with the word to be sure they can use it in context.)

- Use mnemonics or other memory devices (e.g., There's *a rat* in sep*arat*e).

Facilitate Success on Spelling Tests

- Shorten spelling lists and include only the most important words for memorization.

- If spelling tests include dictated sentences, let students know the sentences in advance so they can practice them.

- Allow extra time on spelling tests.

- Keep in mind that it does students no good to learn words for a weekly test if they cannot spell them in real-life situations.

Spelling in Other Content Areas

- Take steps to make sure that poor spelling does not hinder students' development in other areas.

- Don't penalize students for misspelled words in other content area subjects.

- Teach students to use electronic spell-checkers.

- Provide poor spellers with dictionaries in which words are entered according to how they sound.

- Encourage students to keep personal spelling charts with words that give them the most difficulty.

- Post frequently-needed, hard-to-spell words and the most important spelling rules/patterns with examples in the classroom for quick reference.

- Encourage students to say a word slowly and spell it inaudibly before attempting to write it.

- Teach students to write a word several times on scratch paper to see what "looks right."

- Have students circle words they are unsure of so they can return to the words later. This way the flow of their writing will not be interrupted.

- Always analyze students' work to plan future spelling instruction.

Written Composition

Basic Considerations

- Provide explicit instruction in written composition. Skills like selecting a topic, organizing a piece, developing mood, choosing appropriate words, creating figurative language, etc., do not come naturally to many students.

- Provide brief, structured lessons with immediate applications.

- Motivate students to feel ownership for their writing. Give them choices of topic selection and show respect for their ideas and feelings.

- Give real purposes for writing.

- Integrate writing with other content areas.

- Call students' attention to only a few errors at a time (i.e., the most important ones).

- Give advanced notice of writing assignments.

- Provide more time to do writing assignments.

- Shorten assignments when necessary.

- Read examples of classic literature and good writing and discuss the characteristics that make the writing effective.

- Read examples of poor, disjointed writing and contrast with good writing.

Process Writing

Most students benefit from using process writing for written composition (Calkins 1994; Graves 1994). Process writing has stages that are recursive. In other words, students can return to an earlier writing stage at any point.

Some advantages of process writing are:

✔ It eliminates the pressure of producing a perfect paper early in the writing process.

✔ Students are free to think about purposes and meaning before having to worry about mechanics.

✔ It provides peer interaction and discussion of the writing process, which facilitates learning.

✔ It is highly individualized because students can work at different rates and in different ways.

✔ It is a process that good writers naturally go through as they develop a piece.

Here are the five stages of process writing:

1. Prewriting Stage

Students activate prior knowledge. They brainstorm topics and accompanying ideas. They may organize their ideas in a graphic organizer (visual chart or diagram). They can do preliminary reading or research and discuss with others to extend their own ideas.

2. Drafting Stage

Students put their ideas down on paper without paying too much attention to language mechanics or format. They are mostly concerned with conveying their intended meanings to the audience.

3. Sharing/Revising for Meaning

Students usually read their pieces to a peer or to the teacher who asks questions and makes comments regarding meaning. Students then revise for meaning. Correct language mechanics and format are still relatively unimportant.

4. Sharing/Revising for Language Mechanics and Format

After making sure the meaning is clear, students share the composition with peers or the teacher again. This time they discuss spelling, grammar, legibility, etc. Then they revise one last time as they write their final copy. This is the stage where they need to be sure words are spelled correctly, use their best handwriting or computer skills, and make sure papers are neat and organized.

5. Publishing

During the final stage, students share their compositions as final products. They may do this through reading compositions to peers, publishing in class books, putting the published piece in their writing portfolios, publishing on a class Web page, etc.

Hints for Successful Process Writing

- Initially, work through the writing process using a whole-class writing experience in which the class goes through the stages together to write one composition.

- Help students develop a positive self-image of themselves as writers. Help them feel ownership by allowing choices and individualization.

- As students work in other areas, have them jot down good ideas to write about later. Keep these in a writing folder.

- Don't rush through the prewriting stage. Don't let students settle on topics too quickly.

- On the other hand, if students are stuck and can't seem to get started with the first draft, try timing it. Tell them they only have ten minutes to get all their major ideas down in some fashion.

- Ask students to write on every other line during the drafting and revising stages. This gives them room to make corrections without having to completely recopy a piece every time.

- Emphasize that peers can only make suggestions and comments about a composition. The writer is the one who makes decisions about revisions.

- Teach peers to respond constructively. They should always begin by saying something positive.

- Teach simple editing marks and provide a checklist to guide editing.

- When works are published, teach classmates to respond with thoughtful comments about what they liked so authors will feel good about their work.

- Remind students they can return to an earlier writing stage at any point, if needed. For example, as students share with peers, they may realize that the meaning is unclear or incomplete, so they may choose to go back to the prewriting stage to think of more ideas to include.

- Be a writer yourself. Model every stage of process writing and explain your reasoning.

- Provide writing frames. For example, provide a model composition to follow as students change characters, settings, etc.

- Some students may need to audiotape compositions first for later transcription. In some cases, someone other than the student with dysgraphia may need to transcribe the piece.

- Allow students to occasionally work together as co-authors.

Journaling

- Encourage students to keep a journal where they regularly write their thoughts. Here are four types:

1. **Personal Journals** — students record personal thoughts about events at school and at home

2. **Reader-Response Journals** — students read literature and respond to it

3. **Dialogue/Conversation Journals** — students engage in dialogues with teachers, parents, or friends; should be similar to written conversations

4. **Learning Logs** — students respond to what they are studying in content area subjects; for example, explaining math procedures, responding to historical scenarios, or self-assessing progress in science

Journaling Tips

- Even students with very poor writing abilities can keep journals. Allow them to use a combination of words and pictures.

- In the beginning you may need to guide students to write journal entries through open-ended questions. As they become accustomed to writing in journals, give them less guidance.

- Use journals to encourage critical and creative thinking. Don't waste valuable journal time by having students respond to literal questions.

- Make journaling risk-free. Don't grade entries for spelling, grammar, and handwriting. Simply note mistakes in language mechanics for future instruction.

- Collect journals on a regular basis and respond to them with positive written comments. Students will put much more effort into writing their entries if they know the teacher will read them and respond.

- Monitor dialogue journals shared with peers to make sure students are discussing appropriate topics.

- Don't tell students in advance when you plan to collect their journals. This encourages them to keep up with their entries regularly.

- Don't require so much journaling that students become bored or uninterested. They can write in journals daily or a few days a week. They can use one learning log for all content areas or keep a math log the first semester, a science log the second semester, etc.

- Respect confidentiality. Remember that writing is good therapy for many students. Sometimes they just need to vent or express strong feelings in their journals. Tell them that if they record an entry that they do not want you to read that they may fold it over lengthwise and staple it.

- If a student consistently folds and staples entries, talk with him/her. There might be a more serious problem or the student might not be putting effort into writing entries.

Summary ....

People with dysgraphia have extreme difficulties in handwriting, spelling, and/or written composition. Dysgraphia may or may not be accompanied by dyslexia, and it comes in many forms. It's unclear exactly how many students have dysgraphia, but research indicates written language disabilities are very prevalent in students with learning disabilities and that these problems persist.

Writing difficulties affect all areas of school and life. Analyze the specific types of difficulties that students have so you can plan appropriate, individualized instruction. As with other language processing disorders, instruction should be systematic, cumulative, and explicit. It should also be multisensory and take place in meaningful contexts. Put emphasis on remediation so students overcome weaknesses. When remediation is not possible in specific areas, students should learn to compensate for or circumvent their difficulties.

The Source for Learning Disabilities
Copyright © 2000 LinguiSystems, Inc.

References and Resources . . . .

Berninger, V., "The Write Stuff for Preventing and Treating Writing Disabilities," *Perspectives*, 25(2), International Dyslexia Association, Baltimore, 1999.

Calkins, L., *The Art of Teaching Writing*, Heineman, Exeter, NH, 1994.

Cicci, R., *What's Wrong with Me?*, Baltimore Press, New York, 1995.

Graham, S., Harris, K., MacArthur, C., and Schwartz, S., "Writing Instruction," In B. Wong (Ed.) *Learning About Learning Disabilities*, Academic Press, San Diego, CA, 1991.

Graves, D., *Writing: Teachers and Children at Work*, Heineman, Exeter, NH, 1994.

Jordan, D., *Overcoming Dyslexia in Children, Adolescents, and Adults*, ProEd, Austin, TX, 1995.

Hammill, D. and Bartel, N., *Teaching Students with Learning and Behavior Problems*, ProEd, Austin, TX, 1995.

Hochman, J., "Composition: Expressive Language and Writing." In J. Birsch (Ed.), *Multisensory Teaching of Basic Language Skills*, Brookes, Baltimore, 1999.

"Just the Facts: Spelling," International Dyslexia Association, Baltimore, 1998.

"Just the Facts: What is Dysgraphia?" International Dyslexia Association, Baltimore, 1999.

Levine, M., *Educational Care: A System for Understanding and Helping Children with Learning Problems at Home and in School*, Educator's Publishing Service, Cambridge, 1994.

Moats, L., *Spelling: Development, Disability, and Instruction*, York Press, Baltimore, 1995.

Thurber, D., *D'Nealian Handwriting*, Scott Foresman, Glenview, IL, 1993.

. . . .

The International Dyslexia Association
8600 La Salle Rd, Chester Bld., Suite 382
Baltimore, MD 21286-2044
410-296-0232 or 200-222-3123   <www.interdys.org>

Washington Educational Telecommunications Association (WETA)
P. O. Box 2626
Washington, D.C. 20013
703-998-3293

LD OnLine Tech Guide
<www.ldonline.com/ld_indepth/technology/product_list/writing.html>

6

Dyscalculia

Alfredo is eighteen years old, and he excels in drama and art. He's an avid reader and writes poems and short stories in his spare time. However, he is unable to graduate with his senior class because he doesn't have the required credits in mathematics. Although he has normal intelligence, Alfredo has consistently done poorly in mathematics since primary school. After intensive tutoring and years of practice, he has finally become somewhat competent at basic facts and operations, but he has no idea how or when to apply them. When taking a math test, he simply takes numbers from each problem and inserts them in the algorithms that he memorized when studying for the test. He always carries his personal telephone book in his book bag because he can't remember his own phone number or those of his friends.

Like Alfredo, many people have problems in learning mathematics. The nature of their problems vary. Some students can master basic facts but can't do higher mathematics. Some can do higher math but can't master basics. Some can follow math procedures one day but are unable to follow them the next day. Others may perform mathematical algorithms well in one situation but can't apply them to new situations. Math disabilities can be very frustrating due to the complexity and variety of problems.

Definition

Dyscalculia is a neurological disorder that affects a person's ability to learn and do mathematical problems. It originates as a genetic or congenital disorder of the brain. When a person has dyscalculia, a severe discrepancy exists between general cognitive level and mathematical abilities (Kosc 1974; Rourke and Conway 1997; Sharma 1990; Weedon 1992).

Dyscalculia is divided into subtypes in various ways. Here is a well-known typing worthy of consideration (Kosc 1974):

verbal dyscalculia • difficulties in retrieving/naming math symbols, terms, etc.

practognostic dyscalculia • problems applying math concepts using pictures or manipulatives

lexical dyscalculia • impaired reading of math vocabulary and symbols

graphical dyscalculia • poor writing of math symbols, terms, etc.

ideognostical dyscalculia • difficulty with math conceptualizations

operational dyscalculia • impaired ability to do math operations such as addition, subtraction, multiplication, and division

People with dyscalculia may have a combination of subtypes, which can make identification and treatment perplexing. To further complicate matters, problems with math can be due to other factors that may or may not coexist with dyscalculia. These factors include:

- lack of prerequisite experiences and skills needed for math (e.g., background knowledge, hands-on experiences with numbers)
- mathematical instruction that is inadequate or does not match learning style
- non-mathematical learning disabilities
- below-average intelligence
- math anxiety
- lack of motivation
- failure to perceive mathematics as valuable

Language Deficits

Learning mathematical vocabulary, concepts, symbols, signs, and operations can be hindered by difficulties similar to those that hinder language processing ("Curriculum" 1989). For example, people with language processing disabilities usually have problems with directionality, sequencing, and organization. Mathematical algorithms require working in an organized fashion, managing specific directions, and performing steps in the correct order.

Additionally, people with dyslexia have problems with reading, which can make decoding and comprehending mathematical language (e.g., vocabulary, symbols, signs, word problems) challenging. People with handwriting, spelling, and/or written composition disabilities might find mathematical written work difficult. Persons who have trouble expressing themselves orally will have difficulties explaining mathematics aloud, and those with listening problems might have trouble understanding mathematical skills and concepts presented orally. As a result, people are sometimes diagnosed with dyscalculia when the real problem is language processing.

The nature of mathematics is complex because there are multiple domains (e.g., algebra, arithmetic, geometry), which have many subdomains (e.g., arithmetic: place value, basic facts, operations). Less attention has been given to dyscalculia than language disability; there is a relatively small body of knowledge regarding its etiology, incidence, and treatment. So keep in mind that it is sometimes hard to determine if math difficulties are true dyscalculia. A lot of mathematical research does not make the distinction between dyscalculia and math problems that may be due to other factors.

Incidence

As with other learning disabilities, reports of dyscalculia's prevalence vary depending upon the definition and situation. However, research suggests that its prevalence is at least 6% of the school-aged population (Badian 1983, 1999; Kosc 1974). Specifically, Badian reports a prevalence rate of 6.9% with 3.9% of these students low in arithmetic only, and 3% of these students low in arithmetic and reading (1999). He suggests that researchers differentiate between children with arithmetic difficulties and those with both arithmetic and reading problems, in order to prevent distorted interpretations of research.

Characteristics . . . .

Refer to the chart on page 109 for characteristics of dyscalculia that pertain to major difficulties, information processing deficits, and math anxiety. There are many other characteristics that affect a person's ability to compute, conceptualize, or apply mathematics to word problems and real life. For a more detailed listing, see the screening checklist in the next section.

Major Difficulties	Information Processing Deficits	Math Anxiety
lack of sufficient skills in math fundamentals (errors in basics, failure to notice math signs and symbols, etc.)	**attention deficits** (problems paying attention to instruction, can't stay focused on math steps)	intense fear and avoidance of mathematics causes inability to learn math concepts and skills or perform well on math tests
inability to conceptualize and execute math processes (can do correct computation, but students don't understand *why* a strategy worked, so they can't transfer knowledge to new problems)	**visual-spatial deficits** (lose place on worksheets; can't differentiate between numerals, symbols, coins, clock hands, etc.; problems writing in straight lines, aligning numerals, and moving in correct direction; difficulties using the number line)	influence on students' choices of courses in school and careers
Sharma 1990	**auditory processing deficits** (problems with oral drills, etc.)	contributing factors: negative experiences with math in early years, previous failures in math, parent or teacher pressure, poor self-esteem, emphasis on time when performing math, belief in myths (e.g., "Some people have math minds," or "Women are not good at math.")
	memory problems (forget math facts, steps in algorithms, etc.; difficulties solving problems with numerous steps; do poorly on review lessons)	specific: experience stress about particular math situations rather than all math situations
	motor disabilities (write numerals slowly, inaccurately, and illegibly; problems writing numerals in small spaces)	global: feel incompetent in all math situations and dislike all aspects of mathematics intensely
	Miller and Mercer 1997	*Kogelman and Warren 1978 Bitner, Austin, Wadlington 1994 Sharma 1990*

Screening ....

Screening for dyscalculia can be difficult because students may have many or only a few characteristics, and these characteristics range from mild to severe. Other problems such as dyslexia, dysgraphia, or attention deficit disorder can compound the problem or result in a misdiagnosis.

Use the checklist on pages 111-112 to screen for math problems. Check the column that indicates the frequency of the directly observed or reported behavior. Tally the number and frequency that the behaviors occur. Consider characteristics indicative of a learning disability only when inappropriate for the child's age, level of instruction, etc. Because mathematics is so complex and multi-faceted, this checklist doesn't try to name every characteristic—consider it a starting point instead. Also look at data from other sources, such as written work, tests, and interviews. If screening indicates the possibility of dyscalculia, a team (e.g., teachers, psychologists, parents, the student) familiar with the person's work should conduct more intense evaluation.

The Source for Learning Disabilities
Copyright © 2000 LinguiSystems, Inc.

Dyscalculia Screening Checklist

Name_____

Seldom = S   Frequently = F   Always = A

Characteristic	S	F	A
difficulty with one-to-one correspondence			
problems with sequencing (e.g., counting, operations, time, schedules, ideas)			
difficulty with cardinality			
difficulty with ordinality			
difficulty with classification			
lack of number sense (e.g., innate sense that 1,000,000 is much bigger than 1000, or if you add an object to a set, then the set is larger)			
difficulty understanding quantity			
inability to visually cluster (e.g., recognize a small number of objects through observation, rather than counting)			
problems recognizing patterns			
problems with spatial relationships			
problems with temporal relationships			
problems with figure-ground relationships			
problems visualizing mathematics concepts nonverbally			
lack of estimation skills			
inability to recognize equivalence			
difficulty with visual and/or auditory discrimination			
inability to conserve (e.g., number, length, mass, weight, area, volume)			
inability to relate parts to wholes or wholes to parts			
inability remember basic facts or procedures			
inability to perform basic operations			
inability to choose correct procedures			
inability to work in correct direction when performing math calculations			
counting on fingers			
inability to do simple mental arithmetic			
whispers as performs math work			
inability to transfer numerals from one form to another (e.g., 30 = thirty)			
reverses numerals, symbols, etc.			
leaves numerals out (e.g., 22 for 252)			
perseverates numerals (e.g., 4444 for 44)			
misaligns written numerals on paper			
writes sloppy, illegible math papers			
confuses mathematical signs and symbols (e.g., =, +, x, >, <, $)			
makes numerous, careless errors			

Dyscalculia Screening Checklist, *cont.*   Name_____

Seldom = S   Frequently = F   Always = A

Characteristics	S	F	A
can memorize basics but can't apply to higher-level mathematics			
understands higher-level math but can't remember basics			
problems with short-term memory			
problems with active working memory			
problems with long-term memory			
difficulty maintaining attention to mathematics			
inability to choose or focus on important details			
inability to relate concrete manipulatives to mathematical ideas			
difficulty with abstractions (e.g., continues to need manipulatives long after other students discard them)			
lacks ability to reason mathematically (i.e., deductive or inductive)			
difficulty putting mathematical ideas into words, or difficulty understanding mathematical ideas when expressed verbally			
difficulty reading word problems			
approaches solving word problems unsystematically			
difficulty generalizing mathematics to new situations, other academic areas, and/or real life			
difficulty monitoring own thinking processes (i.e., metacognition)			
continues to use mathematical procedures that are no longer appropriate			
tries to memorize mathematics rather than truly learn concepts			
does not know if an answer to a problem is logical			
cannot use calculators or computers for mathematics			
lacks fluency or automatization in mathematical performance			
inconsistency in mathematical performance			
experiences math anxiety and avoidance			
acts bored or unmotivated regarding mathematics			
works mathematical problems very slowly			
experiences extreme fatigue or frustration when doing mathematics			
achievement in mathematics is significantly below potential			

- Student appears to have most of the above problems in:

  _____ concepts

  _____ computation

  _____ application to word problems or real life

The Source for Learning Disabilities

Intervention . . . .

When planning instruction and intervention, keep in mind two types of mathematics learning personalities: quantitative and qualitative (Sharma 1990).

Quantitative

People with *quantitative* learning personalities:

- are sequentially-oriented
- are good in language
- like to solve problems component-by-component
- like to take a problem apart, solve each piece, and put it back together
- are good at quantifying information and solving word problems in a very organized, sequenced, logical fashion
- are more part-to-whole oriented (i.e., bottom up)
- have trouble perceiving holistic relationships among concepts/procedures
- learn best through deductive, structured, step-by-step methods; prefer one standard strategy to solve problems

Qualitative

People with *qualitative* learning personalities:

- are more likely to focus on the visual/spatial, holistic, and inductive aspects of mathematics
- use intuitive approaches in solving problems
- learn mathematics by perceiving patterns and general relationships between concepts and procedures
- eliminate steps, invent new ways to solve problems, and are more whole-to-part oriented (i.e., top down)
- have difficulties following sequences and with attention to detail, often resulting in careless errors, lack of automaticity in fundamentals, and work that appears sloppy
- often find geometry easier to learn than other mathematical concepts
- learn best through inductive, visual-spatial, and pattern recognizing strategies; able to simultaneously consider several strategies or concepts at one time

Quantitative and qualitative approaches should be integrated, even though one type of math personality usually remains dominant for the student. Math instructors should use deductive and inductive instruction; standard sequential, organized, procedural methods; and visual, spatial, and pattern recognition methods.

NCTM Standards

Base mathematics instruction on the *Curriculum and Evaluation Standards of the National Council of Teachers of Mathematics* ("Curriculum" 1989). According to this document, all students in kindergarten through twelfth grades should:

- learn to value mathematics
- become confident in their ability to do mathematics
- become mathematical problem solvers
- be able to communicate mathematically
- learn to reason mathematically

The curriculum is divided into standards for grades K-4 , 5-8, and 9-12. The standards build on each other, are interrelated, and permeate the curriculum. Bear in mind that the *Standards* make little reference to learning disabilities, so they may need to be modified to specifically fit the needs of students with dyscalculia (Mastropieri, et. al. 1995).

Requisites

Difficulties in certain requisites can hinder mathematical development. Carefully assess your students to provide instruction in any of the following areas in which they display weaknesses (Levine 1993).

- ✔ Number Concepts
- ✔ Basic Operations
- ✔ Graphomotor Implementation
- ✔ Transfer of Knowledge
- ✔ Mathematical Linguistics
- ✔ Visualization
- ✔ Problem Solving
- ✔ Estimation
- ✔ Active Working Memory and Mental Arithmetic
- ✔ Higher-Order Cognition
- ✔ Depth of Knowledge and Facility
- ✔ Attention to Detail

Intervention Strategies . . . .

The following strategies cover diverse weaknesses. Choose the ones that match the needs of your students. Discuss the advantages and disadvantages of the strategies with your students. Often they can create good strategies of their own.

Structure and Sequence

- Make instruction structured and well organized.

- New concepts should build on old ones. Use the following sequence:
    1. Teach concepts using concrete objects.
    2. Move to pictures, diagrams, and other visuals to represent concepts.
    3. Present concepts abstractly. Students may need to revert to concrete objects or visuals when material is unfamiliar or exceptionally difficult.

Choosing Textbooks and Materials

- Teach the main mathematical concepts thoroughly rather than covering multiple, less important ideas too briefly.

- Explicitly teach mathematical strategies that can be applied to many problems.

- Materials should allow for scaffolding. Teach students concepts initially with ample teacher guidance and support. This guidance and support should be gradually withdrawn as students learn to work independently.

- Although new skills will initially be taught in isolation, integrate them with other known skills.

- Curriculum should provide instruction and practice in prerequisite skills needed for later ones.

- Materials should provide for review that occurs over time, is cumulative, promotes generalization, and encourages fluency (Dixon 1994).

Math Tutors

- Effective tutors should:
    ✔ be highly proficient in their own understanding and use of mathematics

✔ be knowledgeable and have experience with children with learning disabilities

✔ have a firm understanding of child development and know sound instructional teaching strategies

✔ analyze the problems that students are having, and plan realistic goals and interventions

✔ communicate mathematics in language and ways that children can understand

✔ develop good rapport with the students they tutor

Error Pattern Analysis

- If students have problems with computation, conduct error pattern analysis to find specific computation mistakes to remediate (Ashlock 1990).

- Use the following list to classify the many kinds of errors. Modify this error list to fit the patterns of your students.

  ✔ **Basic Fact Error** — does not recall basic facts correctly

  ✔ **Wrong Operation** — uses the wrong operation to solve the problem

  ✔ **Defective Algorithm** — makes mistakes in carrying out an algorithm

  ✔ **Regrouping Error** — makes mistakes in regrouping for operations

  ✔ **Directional Error** — works in the wrong direction

  ✔ **Sequencing Error** — performs steps in the wrong sequence

  ✔ **Conceptual Error** — doesn't understand the basic concepts behind the computations

  ✔ **Copying Error** — copies the problem incorrectly from the text

  ✔ **Recording Error** — gets the right answer but records it incorrectly

  ✔ **Random Response** — the response does not appear to be related to the problem

Math Anxiety

- Help students develop positive math attitudes.

- Provide daily mathematical successes.

- Use easy, interesting problems that students can relate to their daily lives.

- Personalize word problems using students' names, favorite stories, movies, etc.

- Play simple math games.

- Try to make mathematics class risk-free. Don't embarrass or punish children who perform poorly.

- Emphasize learning rather than perfection.

- Help students see their own progress.

- Help each student become an expert in one aspect of mathematics, no matter how small; for example, basic addition facts, lining up problems correctly, diagramming word problems.

- Ask people who have overcome math anxiety to share their experiences with the class.

- Help students recall other areas of life in which they have had difficulties but persevered to do well. Praise students for effort and progress.

Using Manipulatives

- Have your students use manipulatives (concrete objects) to demonstrate mathematical concepts and procedures. Here are some suggestions:

    ✔ counters (beans, poker chips, buttons, etc.)
    ✔ abacus
    ✔ number line
    ✔ geometric shapes
    ✔ geoboards
    ✔ base-ten blocks
    ✔ inch cubes
    ✔ cuisennaire rods
    ✔ play money and cash register

✔ base-ten charts and sticks

✔ attribute blocks

✔ scales

✔ compass

✔ protractor

✔ tangrams

✔ three-dimensional geometric figures

✔ nonstandard measuring tools (paper clips, unsharpened pencils)

✔ linear measuring tools (meterstick, yardstick, ruler)

✔ volume measuring tools (cups, quarts, liters)

✔ thermometers (Celsius and Fahrenheit)

Mathematical Language

- Teach mathematical vocabulary with concrete examples.

- Teach signs and symbols using manipulatives to illustrate meaning.

- When you explain directions and procedures, break them down into sequenced steps. Have students restate them and work a few examples under your supervision. Post these steps so they can refer back to directions later.

- Allow tape-recording of your directions and procedures so students can go back and listen to the tapes later if needed.

- Encourage students to read word problems aloud, several times if necessary.

- Stress meaning rather than memorization of math language.

- Ask students to verbalize what they are doing as they work problems.

- Have students explain procedures and problems to peers who are having trouble understanding.

- Give many opportunities to use mathematical language in informal conversation.

- Do not let poor reading ability interfere with success. If necessary, read problems aloud or ask the students' peers to read them aloud.

Writing Difficulties

- If students have problems with handwriting or making papers neat and organized, have them do the problems on graph paper so they can line numerals up neatly.

- Demonstrate how to turn lined paper sideways (vertically) under lined paper that is positioned correctly (horizontally) to line up numerals.

- When possible, have students write directly in texts so they don't have to copy problems.

- If this is not possible, have students line their papers up right under problems so they do not have to recopy them.

- Make photocopies of problems so students don't have to copy them from the text.

- Teach positioning of sticky notes beside word problems in the math text so students can show their work.

- Include numerals and mathematical symbols along with the alphabet for handwriting practice.

Word Problems

- Word problems should reflect real life and draw on students' real-life experiences. Word problems should often have more than one way to solve them and more than one right answer. Make sure to integrate mathematics with science, social studies, physical education, and other subject areas.

- Ask students to write their own math word problems using real-life experiences, then exchange problems, critique for clarity, and solve.

- Have students code word problems; for example, underlining needed information, crossing out distracters, and circling the question the problem is asking.

- Teach a simple, heuristic way to solve word problems. Here's a tried-and-true example by Polya (1945).

    1. **Understand the problem.** Read and identify important information; know what the problem is asking.

2. **Devise a plan.** Plan strategies to try, operations to use, ways to check work, etc.

3. **Carry out the plan.** Carry out the plan accurately and systematically.

4. **Look back.** Determine if answers are logical, accurate, and understandable.

- When planning strategies for solving problems, students should:

    ✔ Draw a picture or diagram.

    ✔ Make a model.

    ✔ Work backwards.

    ✔ Restate the problem in a different way.

    ✔ Make a chart.

    ✔ Use visual imagery.

    ✔ Break complex problems into simpler problems.

    ✔ Think of a similar problem.

    ✔ Act it out.

- To help students learn to catch their own mistakes, give them sets of problems, some of which are solved correctly and some of which are not. Let them find and explain the errors.

- Use cooperative groups to facilitate problem solving.

Cooperative Groups

Cooperative grouping allows students with dyscalculia to interact with others to solve math problems. Students learn when they talk and listen to each other, reason aloud, plan strategies, work procedures, and check work together. Cooperative group work is highly motivating and can help build math confidence. When planning your groups, keep the following points in mind:

- The task should be multi-faceted, interesting, and on the appropriate level of difficulty.

- Consider individual personalities, strengths, and weaknesses as well as group dynamics when assigning students to groups.

- Seat people so there is face-to-face communication and interaction.

- Foster and model a cooperative atmosphere.

- Explicitly teach social skills (e.g., how to listen to others, how to disagree politely, how to value diverse personalities and talents).

- Supply plenty of manipulatives and other materials.

- All group members should know they are responsible for making sure all other members understand the task and resolution.

- Do not appoint a leader; explain that any group member may be called upon to explain the task's resolution.

- Give all group members important jobs. Here are some examples:

  - ✔ facilitator
  - ✔ encourager
  - ✔ oral reader
  - ✔ artist
  - ✔ recorder
  - ✔ materials supervisor
  - ✔ timekeeper
  - ✔ checker

- Monitor groups to make sure students are on the right track, everyone is actively involved, and attitudes are helpful.

- Change groups at regular intervals.

Drill and Practice

Students need to memorize basic math facts, if possible. In order to encourage this, remember these tips:

- Break facts into manageable chunks for memorization so students aren't overwhelmed (e.g., the first half of the +2s, then the second half of the +2s, then the first half of the +3s).

- After students master each "chunk," have them practice mixed chunks.

- Give students extra time and practice to work toward mastery.

- Make practice multisensory (say, see, and write facts as they practice).

- Play math games that require recall of facts.

- Teach memory tricks. For example, in the multiplication table for nine, the resulting digits equal the sum of nine (2x9=18, 1+8=9; 3x9=27, 2+7=9).

- Emphasize linking strategies such as turn-around facts (e.g., 3+6, 6+3; 8x5, 5x8) or other numeric relationships (e.g., after learning +10s, remember that the +9s are [n + 9] = [(n+10)-1)]).

- Don't let lack of mastery of basic facts keep students from moving on to higher level concepts. As they continue to work on learning basic facts, teach them how to use number lines, numeral charts, counters, and calculators so they can move to fractions, decimals, geometry, etc.

- Don't press for speed until students have mastered basic facts at a slower pace. Then conduct timed drills with only a few facts at a time. Allow them to time themselves if this helps with math anxiety.

Computers

- Teach how and when to use technology. Computers for mathematics can motivate, provide repeated opportunities for drill and practice, and encourage higher-level thinking. When shopping for math software, look for these characteristics (Babbitt 2000):

  ✔ minimal screen clutter

  ✔ connections with your teaching

  ✔ the ability to modify speed, the number of problems, etc.

  ✔ small increments in difficulty between levels

  ✔ limited number of attempts for each problem

  ✔ helpful, immediate feedback

  ✔ good record-keeping of students' efforts and mastery

  ✔ built-in instructional aides, such as visuals

  ✔ simulation of real-life situations

The Source for Learning Disabilities
Copyright © 2000 LinguiSystems, Inc.

Calculators

Free your students to think critically and creatively by allowing them to use calculators for routine procedures as well as to explore new ideas.

- Explain the following points to parents and others who might question the wisdom of using a calculator:

    ✔ You will still be teaching students basic facts, operations, and mental math.

    ✔ Students recognize that recalling basic facts from memory is quicker than using calculators and will continue to do so when appropriate.

    ✔ Calculators cannot choose operations or other procedures to solve problems. Students will have to understand mathematical concepts and skills to know what to program into calculators.

    ✔ Calculators allow students who have not mastered basic facts and operations to move on to higher-level mathematics.

    ✔ Calculators allow students to explore new concepts and free them to focus on mathematical problem solving rather than rote memorization.

    ✔ In the real world, adults use calculators for many purposes.

Attention and Memory

- Seat students near the focal point of instruction.

- Use multisensory techniques (visual, auditory, tactile, and kinesthetic channels). Subvocalizing is often effective.

- Make learning meaningful and help students connect new ideas to prior knowledge.

- Provide motivating, interesting tasks in environments without disruptions.

- Actively involve students. Lengthy lectures and other passive activities hinder attention, learning, and memory.

- Use mnemonics to aid memory. For example, teach "**P**lease **E**xcuse **M**y **D**ear **A**unt **S**ally" which are the steps in solving an equation (**p**arentheses,

exponents, **m**ultiplication, **d**ivision, **a**ddition, **s**ubtraction).

- Post memory aides in the classroom (basic facts, counting chart, place value chart).

- Encourage making lists and checking off points on the list as they are accomplished.

Math for Everyday Living

You may have some students who will never be gifted mathematicians, but make sure they learn basic math skills needed to function in society. Take into account your students' basic abilities and life situations to determine these essential skills. Here are some suggested situations:

- using money
- telling time
- writing checks and balancing a checkbook
- taking simple measurements
- using a calendar
- using a calculator
- figuring simple percentages and interest
- using estimation
- interpreting simple graphs and charts
- understanding basic statistics found in the daily newspaper

Final Notes

- Frequently observe and interview students to plan instruction.

- Don't allow students to practice errors. Monitor them to catch errors quickly.

- Give plenty of time and opportunities to master concepts and skills.

- Stress concept development and problem solving. Do not overemphasize computation at the expense of other concepts.

- Interact daily with students one-on-one.

- Present and model information in multiple ways. Some students learn best through listening. Some need concepts demonstrated, and some learn best by doing.

- If students fail to master a concept or skill after an appropriate time, use a different teaching method to present it. Don't simply go through the unsuccessful process one more time.

- Give immediate feedback and rewards.

- Break math class up into small segments for presentation of new knowledge, review, and practice. Several short sessions are usually better than one long one.

- Prioritize. Decide what students must know and what would simply be nice to know.

- Set goals with due dates. Have students check off goals on a calendar as they reach them.

- Encourage metacognition. In other words, encourage students to think about their own thought processes and learning. Help them analyze what works and what does not.

- Be flexible and open to new ideas.

- Be patient. Progress may be slow and inconsistent. Have realistic expectations.

- Refer students for additional assessment and intervention if you suspect other problems.

Summary . . . .

Dyscalculia is a neurological learning disability that affects a person's ability to learn and do mathematics. People with dyscalculia are diverse; some are able to memorize basic facts and do simple operations but cannot understand higher level concepts. Others quickly catch on to complex mathematics but cannot seem to master the basics. Dyscalculia may be complicated by other factors such as language processing problems, attention deficit, poor instruction, or lack of motivation. People with dyscalculia often suffer from math anxiety, which is an intense fear and avoidance of mathematics.

Due to the diversity of characteristics, the complexity of mathematics, and the lack of research, many students with dyscalculia often do not get the help they need. Educators and parents need to be aware of characteristics so that they can identify children early. Instruction should move from concrete objects to visual representations to abstract thinking. The use of manipulatives, ample drill and practice, and transfer to real-life problems are mandatory for intervention. The use of calculators and computers can also be very beneficial.

References and Resources . . . .

Ashlock, R., *Error Patterns in Computation*, Merrill, New York, 1990.

Babbit, B. C., "10 Tips for Software Selection for Math Instruction," April 2, 2000, <http://www.ldonline.org/ld_indepth/technology/babbitt_math_tips.html> (April 9, 2000).

Badian, N., "Dyscalculia and Nonverbal Disorders of Learning," In H.R. Myklebust (ed.), *Progress in Learning Disabilities*, Vol. 5., Grune and Stratton, New York, 1983.

Badian, N., "Persistent Arithmetic, Reading, or Arithmetic and Reading Disability," *Annals of Dyslexia*, Vol. 49, 1999, pp. 45-70.

Bitner, J., Austin, S., and Wadlington, E., "A Comparison of Math Anxiety in Traditional and Nontraditional Developmental College Students," *Research and Teaching in Developmental Education*, 10(2), 1994, pp. 35-43.

"Curriculum and Evaluation Standards," National Council of Teachers of Mathematics, Reston, VA, 1989.

Dixon, B., "Research Guidelines for Selecting Mathematics Curriculum," *Effective School Practices*, 13(2), 1994, pp. 47-55.

Kogelman, S. and Warren, J., *Mind Over Math*, McGraw-Hill, New York, 1978.

Kosc, L., "Developmental Dyscalculia," *Journal of Learning Disabilities*, 7(3), 1974, pp. 164-177.

Levine, M., *Developmental Variation and Learning Disorders*, Educators Publishing Service, Cambridge, 1993.

Mastropieri, M., Scruggs, T., and Chung, S., "Instructional Interventions for Students with Mathematics Learning Disabilities," In Wong (Ed.), *Learning about Learning Disabilities*, Academic Press, San Diego, 1995, pp. 445-451.

Miller, S. and Mercer, C., "Educational Aspects of Mathematics Disabilities," *Journal of Learning Disabilities*, 30(1), 1997, pp. 47-56.

Polya, G., *How to Solve It*, Princeton University Press, Princeton, 1945.

Rourke, B. and Conway, J., "Disabilities of Arithmetic and Mathematical Reasoning: Perspective from Neurology and Neuropsychology," *Journal of Learning Disabilities*, 30 (1), 1997, pp. 34-46.

Sharma, M., "NCTM Student Math Notes," National Council of Teachers of Mathematics (NCTM), ED 328 413, Reston, VA, 1990.

Weedon, C., "Specific Learning Difficulties in Mathematics," Department of Education, University of Stirling and Tayside Region, ED 361 944, 1992.

▪ ▪

The International Dyslexia Association
8600 LaSalle Road
Chester Building, Suite 382
Baltimore, MD 21286-2044
410-296-0232 or 800-222-3123
<www.interdys.org>

National Council of Teachers of Mathematics
1906 Association Dr.
Reston, VA 20191-9988
703-620-9840
<www.nctm.org>

National Information Center for Children and Youth with Disabilities
P. O. Box 1492
Washington, D.C. 20013
800-695-0285
<www.nichcy.org>

▪ ▪

Notes

7

Attention Deficit Disorder (ADD)

Dear Mrs. Miller,

Your son is having problems attending. He always knows how to do what we are doing, he just never knows where I am, or what I said when I call on him. It's beginning to affect his grades. I've got him at my side and I've had him there for several weeks. He says he doesn't hear me sometimes, but I have a loud voice. Either he is *deep* into thought, or he has a hearing problem. I feel it's the first. We'll keep working. I love having him in my class—he is so lovable. I'm mainly concerned about how it affects his work.

Mrs. Miller received this note from her son's third-grade teacher after she asked about his performance in school. She had expected to receive a note like this one day. She knew her son had difficulty sitting and listening to classroom discussions, recalling important information, and answering questions orally. He repeated kindergarten because he needed extensive use of manipulatives to understand basic concepts, and he always chose developmental activities that involved gross-motor skills. When he began preschool, his parents reminded him each morning, "Put on your listening ears!" He had difficulty following verbal discussions when the topic involved unfamiliar experiences or abstract concepts. In other words, his weaknesses in language and auditory processing were characterized by attention deficits. There are many children like Mrs. Miller's son—children who have difficulty attending in the classroom and controlling their behavior.

The ability to attend is a skill people must have in order to succeed academically, vocationally, and socially. Those who attend well can acquire and retain information better than those who have difficulty controlling internal and external influences that interfere with thinking and learning, behavior, and interpersonal relationships.

Definition

Medical Definition

The critical feature of Attention Deficit Disorder (ADD) is a consistent pattern of inattention, impulsivity, and/or hyperactivity that occurs more frequently and severely than in other children at a similar level of development (DSM-IV 1994). Many children exhibit these characteristics, but some demonstrate a more prominent pattern of behaviors in one area. The behaviors appear in early childhood, usually before age seven, and persist for at least six months. *The Diagnostic and Statistical Manual of Mental Disorders, Fourth Edition,* subtypes ADD into three groups based on the number of predominant characteristics exhibited and a minimum length of time the behaviors exist.

The Three Types of Attention Deficit/Hyperactivity Disorder

1. *Predominantly Inattention*

- six or more symptoms of inattention, but fewer than six symptoms of hyperactivity-impulsivity for at least six months

2. *Predominantly Hyperactive-Impulsive*

- six or more symptoms of hyperactivity-impulsivity, but fewer than six symptoms of inattention, for at least six months
- inattention continues to be a significant feature

3. *Combined*

- the most common of the three types
- children demonstrate six or more symptoms of inattention and six or more symptoms of hyperactivity-impulsivity for at least six months

---

Symptoms of ADD can change over time. Children originally diagnosed with one subtype of ADD may present with another type as they get older. A predominant symptom may change or diminish. For example, when predominant symptoms (e.g., Attention Deficit/Hyperactivity Disorder, Predominantly Inattention Type) no longer meet the criteria for that subtype, a diagnosis of Attention Deficit/Hyperactivity Disorder, in Partial Remission is given. Attention Disorder/Hyperactivity Not Otherwise Specified is used when persons exhibit symptoms of ADD, but none of the criteria for any of the subtypes are met (DSM-IV 1994). Ongoing assessment of behavior by teachers, family members, and medical personnel is essential to a correct diagnosis and effective intervention.

Educational Definition

The U.S. Department of Education includes children with ADHD under the Other Health Impairments (OHI) category of IDEA Amendments of 1997 ("Legal Issues" 2000). OHI result in reduced efficiency in educational performance or in one or more student life activities. Chronic and acute health impairments such as heart conditions, tuberculosis, rheumatic fever, sickle cell anemia, epilepsy, leukemia, diabetes, and ADD are included under OHI. Children suspected of having a health impairment should receive a multidisciplinary

Characteristics of ADD:

- marked by degrees of inattention, impulsivity, and hyperactivity

- developmental disorder that persists throughout adulthood

- difficult to find consistent incidence numbers

- males affected more than females

- some inheritance links

evaluation. An evaluation should minimally include a medical examination, an educational evaluation, and a family interview.

Incidence

Incidence data for ADD is inconsistent because of differences in assessment such as definition of the disorders, criteria, evaluators' expertise, even though ADD is "the most commonly diagnosed childhood behavioral disorder" ("ADHD Newly Diagnosed" 2000). It's estimated that at least 20% of children with learning disabilities have difficulty attending ("Learning Disabilities" 2000), and 3-5% of all school-aged children have ADD (DSM-IV 1994).

A child who has a parent with ADD is more likely to be diagnosed with ADD (DSM-IV 1994; "Fact Sheet" 2000). The disorder occurs much more frequently in males than in females. Some incidence figures indicate male:female ratios range from 4:1 to as high as 9:1 (DSM-IV 1994).

A common myth of ADD is that over time, a person will outgrow it. However, ADD is a developmental disorder that persists throughout adulthood. Behaviors continue into adolescence for 50-80% of children diagnosed with ADD, and 30-50% still have ADD as adults ("Attention Deficit Disorder" 2000). Research reveals that the behaviors become less noticeable as the child matures, and the stereotypical gross motor behaviors (e.g., running everywhere, can't sit still) may be replaced with forgetfulness and difficulty following conversations or discussions.

Characteristics . . . .

Children with ADD demonstrate behaviors that consistently occur more frequently and significantly than in children of the same developmental age. The behaviors are significant enough that they have a negative impact on a child's home, social, and school settings, and on an adult's work and independent living environment.

There are three major characteristics of ADD:

- distractibility or inattention

- impulsivity or lack of impulse control

- hyperactivity or excessive physical activity and restlessness

Characteristics of ADD

Distractibility	Impulsivity	Hyperactivity
makes careless mistakes	interrupts others	leaves seat in classroom
difficulty sustaining attention over a period of time	blurts out answers to questions before questions have been fully given	talks excessively
loses or forgets important things	difficulty waiting his/her turn	fidgety, restless, squirms
difficulty shifting from one activity to another; never seems to complete an activity	acts or speaks without thinking of consequences	difficulty engaging in quiet leisure activities that require attention
doesn't seem to be listening even when spoken to directly	begins tasks without having instructions (e.g., says "I know what to do")	enjoys physical sports as a recreational or leisure activity
easily distracted by unimportant auditory or visual stimuli	doesn't seem to learn from past experiences	inappropriately physically active (e.g., constantly taps pencil, touches everything in the doctor's office)
difficulty adapting to changes in routine	grabs objects from others' hands in order to "see them," "play with them"	accident-prone
lacks ability to plan ahead	described as "impatient"	described as someone who never seems to stop

Screening . . . .

Screen children for ADD to identify those who frequently demonstrate atypical behavior for children their own age. Use the checklist on page 135 to identify behaviors associated with ADD. Note the setting in which the behaviors occur and the name of the person who observes or reports the behaviors. The checklist categorizes the commonly occurring behaviors of ADD under the three major areas: distractibility, impulsivity, and hyperactivity. The rater should tally the frequency of the behavior's occurrence in each area. Do not use the checklist as an instrument for *diagnosis* of ADD.

Use a team approach for diagnosis. Information from the checklist may help team members diagnose the presence of the disorder and its subtype. Parents, teachers, school psychologists, and the child's health-care provider are valuable members of the assessment team. Team members should collect information from a variety of sources and conduct observations over a period of time in a variety of settings.

Check the column that indicates the frequency with which the behavior occurs. The behavior can be directly observed or reported. Tally the number and frequency that the behaviors occur for each section and for all three sections. Share the information with other professionals who may recommend additional testing.

ADD Screening Checklist

Name_____

Seldom = S   Frequently = F   Always = A

Behavior	S	F	A
Distractibility			
has difficulty sustaining attention			
has difficulty listening when spoken to directly			
fails to complete tasks			
has trouble organizing materials and self			
is distracted by environmental stimuli			
loses necessary materials			
tunes out and daydreams			
other:			
Total			
Impulsivity			
talks out of turn			
answers question before the question has been completed			
has difficulty waiting			
interrupts others when speaking			
difficulty maintaining the topic of conversation			
unaware of consequences of actions			
easily frustrated			
grabs objects from others			
other:			
Total			
Hyperactivity			
is frequently in motion, or "on the go"			
talks incessantly			
has difficulty remaining seated			
fidgets or squirms			
has feelings of restlessness			
prefers physical activities			
physically active beyond appropriate time limits			
other:			
Total			
Total number of behaviors			

Intervention . . . .

The following is a summary of the National Attention Deficit Disorder Association's guiding principles for comprehensive assessment, diagnosis, and treatment of ADD ("Guiding Principles" 2000):

1. Evaluate and treat the whole person.

ADD affects the physical, social, academic, and vocational aspects. Conduct assessment and treatment across all affected areas.

2. ADD should be suspected, but not presumed.

ADD commonly coexists with a learning disability, but it can be present in the absence of a learning disability. In other words, not everyone with ADD has a learning disability.

3. ADD may present across the life span.

ADD is a developmental disorder that occurs in early childhood and can persist through adulthood. Symptoms may diminish or change as the person ages.

4. A comprehensive assessment is necessary for an accurate diagnosis.

An assessment should evaluate the whole person, but answers to certain questions help the assessment team make a more accurate diagnosis. Some questions that differentiate the subtypes of ADD might include: What is the frequency of the behaviors? At what age did the symptoms appear? Are there any other physical or emotional explanations for the behaviors?

5. Qualified professionals should conduct evaluation and treatment of ADD.

A team of qualified professionals (including the parents, teachers, therapists, and health-care providers) should conduct the evaluation. These people should have training and experience working with people with ADD.

6. Response to medication should not be used as the basis to diagnose ADD.

ADD is a disorder characterized by a number of behaviors that exist for a certain period of time. The diagnosis is not based on how the behaviors change as the result of medication. People with and without ADD respond to the same medication in different ways.

7. Diagnosis should be based primarily on DSM-IV criteria.

The National ADDA recommends that criteria for the diagnosis of ADD be standardized. Standardization may increase the accuracy of the diagnosis and allow for more valid and reliable data collection.

8. Diagnosis and treatment should involve people familiar with the person.

Professionals often diagnose people with ADD without observing them in their environment or talking extensively with teachers, parents, or spouse. ADD is a pervasive developmental disorder that requires a comprehensive team assessment and includes people most familiar with the person being evaluated.

9. Treatment should involve multiple disciplines.

Effective intervention typically includes behavior modification and accommodations and modifications to the educational curriculum. Medication may also be a viable form of treatment. Consider all aspects of the intervention plan within a collaborative team model.

10. Practitioners should know current research and diagnostic tools.

Professionals who assess and treat people with ADD have an ethical responsibility to be knowledgeable about the disorder and to be familiar with current diagnostic instruments and treatment techniques. Many states and professional associations require professionals to obtain continuing education units (CEUs) in order to maintain their licenses or certificates to practice. Attend conventions, take in-service training, and engage in professional development activities (e.g., reading journals, writing articles, giving presentations) to learn further ADD assessment and intervention techniques.

Intervention Strategies · · · · · · · · · · · · · · · · · · ·

Most people with ADD are easily distracted and have short attention spans. A good over-all intervention plan raises awareness and modifies social behaviors that can negatively affect intrapersonal feelings and interfere with interpersonal relationships.

The strategies in this section increase attention while reducing impulsivity and hyperactivity. They are listed under three main accommodation and modification areas: environmental, instructional, and social. Strategies can fit into more than one area. A special section on medications that increase attention and decrease hyperactivity is found on pages 143, and some alternative explanations for ADD are on 144.

Environmental

Engineer, or plan and design the environment to meet the needs of students with disabilities.

General

- Survey the environment.

- Evaluate the physical layout of the room in relation to where students work.

- Make changes that will help focus attention.

Schedule

- Post schedules, rules, and consequences. Write them on the board or on a card displayed at the students' desks.

- Follow a predictable schedule. When schedule changes occur, give ample warning and preparation. Give repeated announcements when the time for a schedule change approaches.

- Schedule a time each day for physical activities. Students with ADD benefit from gross-motor activities. Competition-free activities may be the best choice (e.g., swinging, hitting a tennis ball against a backboard).

Seating

- Allow preferential seating.

- Seat students near the teacher or with peers who are on-task, but seat them away from distracters (e.g., bulletin boards and storage cabinets).

- Ensure that the student can see the board or overhead projector.

- Provide alternative seating if necessary.

Create New Spaces

- Create learning centers or work stations for individual or small group work.

- Provide a study carrel.

- Create an area in the classroom or school that provides a quiet, safe place where students can reflect and gain control of behavior.

Instructional

Instructional accommodations and modifications increase the likelihood that students will be successfully included in the general education curriculum. Accommodations are the changes in the way a student receives instruction (visual vs. auditory, peer tutoring) or produces work (speaks rather than writes, extended time for test taking). Accommodations support students' strengths while diminishing weaknesses. Modifications adapt, modify, or change a student's academic material from the work required from other students in the same class. Outline accommodations and modifications on the students' individual education programs (IEP).

General

- Reduce the length of assignments or tasks.

- Provide extra time for assignments, tests, etc.

- Practice test-taking strategies such as skimming text for information, highlighting facts, and outlining main ideas and related concepts. (These reduce required reading and writing—weaknesses exhibited by many students with ADD.)

- Tell students about upcoming information. Monitor lesson pace, shorten lecture time, and increase participation time.

- Increase the time to discuss and demonstrate concepts. Use group or unison responses to keep the students on task and to check their comprehension.

- Use attention-getting visual signals such as hand signals, flashing the classroom's lights, and highlighting important information with color.

Instructions

- Give clear, simple instructions.

- Avoid multi-step instructions.

- Repeat instructions when necessary.

- Provide multiple examples with demonstrations.

- Use multisensory manipulatives to supplement verbal instructions.

Make Learning Interesting and Enjoyable

- Ask interesting questions, show pictures, and use computer software and the Internet.

- Hide objects in the classroom or fill a grab bag with objects for an upcoming lesson to create interesting discussions or writing activities (Rief 2000).

- Use mnemonics, rhymes, or songs to aid memory.

- Move around the classroom. It creates interest and you can unobtrusively monitor behavior.

Organization and Materials

- Have students use assignment pads to record the materials required for each assignment.

- Encourage the use of lists to help keep track of required materials and to prioritize and complete tasks.

- Encourage students to color-code book covers and notebooks. Students will locate all of the materials for one subject more quickly if their books' covers and notebooks are the same color.

- Show how to use a calendar to plan short-range and long-range tasks. Have students use a calendar to set goals to meet academic deadlines and social activities.

- Use a single-tabbed binder to file homework and graded papers. Students who have one notebook or binder for each subject are more likely to lose or forget necessary materials.

- Have students regularly check their inventory for frequently-used and required materials. Students with ADD often lose or misplace their belongings.

- Allow the use of word processors and voice recognition software, portable electronic devices (e.g., spell checkers, dictionaries), and personal assistive listening devices. Assistive technology can reduce the stress associated with academic requirements (e.g., spelling and handwriting).

Social

The following strategies can increase socially-appropriate behaviors. Techniques that foster self-awareness and self-monitoring behaviors reduce impulsivity and increase socially-appropriate behaviors. Reinforce inappropriate behaviors with clearly defined, immediately-applied consequences.

General

- Implement a structured behavior management system.

- Consistently follow the behavior plan and reward system.

- Improve time management for social, academic, and vocational activities. Students with ADD often have difficulty recognizing and responding to social cues.

- Give the student and family information about the disorder and where to find support services within the community.

- Encourage involvement in activities that develop socialization and cooperation among peers (e.g., scouting, after school clubs, etc.).

Behavior Plans and Reward Systems

- Use contracts, charts, and a token-economy reward system for appropriate behavior if necessary.

- Establish criteria for rewards (e.g., completing a certain number of items, working for a certain length of time).

- Choose activities and tasks that the student performs well. Reward for success *and* effort.

- Use a timer or buzzer with intermittent beeps. Students can reward themselves if they are on-task when the timer goes off.

Self-Monitoring

- Teach students to self-monitor behavior.

- Have students evaluate their behavior and chart their own performance at the end of an activity or class period.

- Ask students to design their own schedules for in-school tasks and after-school activities. Planning decreases the chances that they will forget about an assignment or appointment, complain that there wasn't enough time to get it done, or wait until the last minute to start a task.

- Have older students write notes to remind themselves of questions rather than asking the questions at an inappropriate time. Use sticky notes or a small notebook kept on desks for quick access.

Verbal Cues and Role Playing

- Provide clear verbal cues. For example, say, "Listen to what your friend is telling you. He asked you to stop interrupting him."

- Keep explanations short and base them on established rules and consequences.

- Role-play social situations and alternative responses.

Medication

One of the most controversial issues in medicine and education is the use of drugs to treat ADD. Professional and popular literature is filled with studies and articles about the frequency with which drugs are prescribed to control children's behavior and the possible side effects of these drugs. *Most professionals agree that medication should not be the only form of treatment.* If medication is prescribed, behavior management and special modifications and accommodations to the environment (academic, home, vocational) can also yield long-term benefits.

Incidence

Data varies on how many school-aged children with ADD take drugs to control behavior—some studies report that as many as 60-90% (ADD: Adding Up the Facts 2000). A study conducted at the University of Maryland-Baltimore found that "the use of Ritalin and other stimulants, which are used to treat attention deficit disorders, increased almost three-fold in the early 1990s" (Shute, et. al. 2000).

Stimulants: Pros and Cons

Stimulants such as Ritalin (methylphenidate), Dexedrine (dextroamphetamine), and Cylert (emoline) are frequently prescribed to treat symptoms of ADD. The intended effect is to stimulate the central nervous system, which results in improved attention, concentration, motor control, and reduced hyperactivity. Information from the National Institute of Mental Health reveals that at least 90% of hyperactive children can be helped with either Ritalin or Dexedrine. The drugs are effective for 3-4 hours and "move out of the body within twelve hours" ("Learning Disabilities" 2000).

Some reported side effects of these drugs include: nervousness, insomnia, loss of appetite, slowed growth, lethargy, moodiness, and addiction. Because the effectiveness of the drugs varies and the side effects can be significant, groups like Parents Against Ritalin have emerged.

Adults with ADD may also benefit from medication. Researchers have found that the same drugs given to children with ADD will reduce distractibility and impulsivity in adults with ADD. The adults report that the drugs improve their organization and performance in their jobs and daily living functions ("Learning Disabilities" 2000).

Alternative Explanations and Treatment for ADD

Researchers are exploring alternative explanations and treatment for symptoms of ADD. Some physicians believe the symptoms are due to hypoglycemia or low blood sugar, allergic reactions or sensitivity to inhalants (e.g., dust, pollen, mold, dust mites), foods, and nutritional deficiencies. In an attempt to stabilize blood sugar, children can be placed on a regime that requires eating smaller meals at shorter intervals. Certain foods can be eliminated from their diet (e.g., refined sugar and dairy products). Vitamins and minerals are recommended as supplements to the diet. Antigen shots can be administered to reduce allergic symptoms. Outcomes of these treatments are debatable. Always speak to the child's physician before adding or deleting certain foods from the diet or before giving dietary supplements.

Auditory Integration Training

Another alternative treatment is Auditory Integration Training (AIT), developed by Dr. Guy Berard. It's designed to help those with behavioral or learning problems. AIT is often used with children with ADD, autism, dyslexia, learning disabilities, and central auditory processing disorders. Berard believes that the behaviors associated with these disorders are attributable to distortions in hearing or auditory processing deficits. Children in AIT receive an audiological evaluation with systematic treatments designed to "normalize hearing" (Auditory Integration Training 2000). Parents, teachers, and students report improvement in the child's social behavior and language with less impulsivity and distractibility. You can assess whether a child might be having problems with his auditory system by completing the Checklist for Parents located on the Internet at <http://www.vision3d.com/adhd/parents.html>.

Team Approach

A team approach to intervention for children with ADD is essential to achieving long-term benefits. Parents, teachers, therapists, and health-care providers should work together to develop strategies to improve behavior, social skills, and academic performance. Information about a student's behavior before and after medication is critical to determining the effectiveness of the medication, its dosage and time of administration, and its side effects. As with any intervention plan, the team must be knowledgeable about the disorder and regularly review and make any necessary revisions to the intervention plan. This is particularly true if medication is a component in the intervention plan for children with ADD.

Summary ....

Attention Deficit Disorder (ADD) and its subtypes are developmental disorders that usually appear in children before age seven and persist for at least six months. Characteristics of the disorder include: forgetfulness, difficulty adapting to changes in routine, acting or speaking without thinking of consequences, being distracted by unimportant auditory or visual stimuli, and inappropriate physical activity.

There are three types of attention deficit disorders: combined, predominately inattention, and hyperactive-impulsive. Assessment should be comprehensive and include a team of professionals who consider the person's social skills, academic or vocational performance, and independent living settings. Intervention strategies are designed to reduce the impact of the disorder across all settings. Academic objectives and benchmarks should reflect, to the greatest extent possible, standards consistent with those of typical students at the same grade level. Appropriate accommodations and modifications to the curriculum should be included on the student's individualized education program (IEP). Medication, a behavior modification program, and the student's educational program may decrease impulsivity, hyperactivity and inappropriate social behaviors, and improve attention and academic performance.

Mrs. Miller's son made this announcement one afternoon when his mother picked him up from after care: "I got a note from my teacher today." Mrs. Miller thought, "Oh no. What now?" He handed his mother a note card:

Mrs. Miller,

Your son has been *wonderful* this week. He has listened to and followed all of my directions. Good job!

Mrs. Miller was beaming, and her son was, too. It was wonderful to know that he attended well and followed his teacher's instructions—and it was also wonderful that his teacher took the time to write a note to let his mother know how well he was doing. Good job!

. . . .

References and Resources . . . .

"ADHD Newly Diagnosed," <http://webmd.lycos.com/content/article/1623.50031> (March 17, 2000).

"Attention Deficit Disorder: Adding Up the Facts," *U.S. Department of Education*, 1994, <http:www.ldonline.org/ ld_indepth/add_adhd/add_doe-facts.html> (March 21, 2000).

"Attention Deficit Disorder: Beyond the Myths," <http://www.ldonline.org/ld_indepth/ add_adhd/add_doe_myths.html> (March 21, 2000).

"Attention Deficit Disorder for Teachers," <http://www.qlink.queensu.ca/~3dw18/add/ add_teachers.html> (March 17, 2000).

Auditory Integration Training and the Counselling Center, March 2000, <http:// www.vision3d.com/adhd/#AIT> (May 17, 2000).

Blazer, B., "Developing 504 Classroom Accommodation Plans: A Collaborative Systematic Parent-Student-Teacher Approach," *Teaching Exceptional Children*," Nov/Dec, 1999, <http://www.ldonline.org/ld_indepth/teaching_techniques/ 504_plans.html> (March 21, 2000).

Block, M. A., *No More Ritalin*: *Treating ADHD Without Drugs*, Kensington Publishing, New York, 1996, <http://www.kensingtonbooks.com> (March 17, 2000).

"Diagnostic and Statistical Manual for Mental Disorders, 4th Ed.," (DSM-IV), American Psychiatric Association, Washington, D.C., 1994.

"Differences in Brain Function Found for Attention Deficit Disorder," <http://www.stan-ford.edu/dept/news/relaged/981123add-h.html> (March 17, 2000).

"Fact Sheet on Attention Deficit Hyperactivity Disorder (ADHD/ADD)," <http://www.add.org/content/abc/factsheet.html> (March 17, 2000).

"Guidelines for the Assessment and Accommodation of Students with Attention Deficit Disorder," <http://www.saonet.ucla.edu/osd/ucdssadd.htm> (March 21, 2000).

"Guiding Principles for the Diagnosis and Treatment of Attention Deficit Hyperactivity Disorder," *The National Attention Deficit Disorder Association*, <http:www.add.org/ gp98.html> (March 17, 2000).

"Learning Disabilities: Decade of the Brain," *National Institute of Mental Health*, <html: www.ldonline.org/ld_indepth/general.info/gen-nimh-booklet.html> (May 2, 2000).

"Legal Issues and ADD," <http://www.add.org/ content/legal1.html> (March 17, 2000).

"Online Attention Deficit Disorder Test: OAD Do You Have ADD?,"
    <http://ww.med.nyu.edu/Psych/addc/addscr.html> (March 17, 2000).

Rief, S., "Checklists for Teachers," from the *ADD Checklist*, reprinted with permission of
    Prentice Hall Direct, 1997, <http://www.ldonline.org/ld_indepth...ng_tech-
    niques/ rief_checklists.html> (March 21, 2000).

Richardson, W., "The Link Between ADD and Addiction: Getting the Help You Deserve,"
    1998, *National Attention Deficit Disorder Association* (*NADDA*), Northbrook, IL, 1998,
    <http://www.add.org/Focus/addiction.html> (March 17, 2000).

Shute, N., Locy, T., and Pasternak, D., "The Perils of Pills: The Psychiatric Medication of
    Children Is Dangerously Haphazard," *U.S. News & World Report*, March, 6, 2000, pp.
    44-50.

■ ■

Attention Deficit Information Network
475 Hillside Avenue
Needham, MA 02194
617-455-9895

Children and Adults with Attention Deficit Disorder (CH.A.D.D.)
8181 Professional Place, Suite 201
Landover, MD 20785
301-306-7070
<www.chadd.org>

Directory of Summer Camps for Children with Learning Disabilities
Learning Disabilities Association of America (LDA)
4156 Library Road
Pittsburgh, PA 15234-1379
412-341-1515
<http://www.ldanatl.org>

National Attention Deficit Disorder Association (NADDA)
P.O. Box 1303
Northbrook, IL 60065-1303
email: mail@add.org

Parents Against Ritalin
225 S. Brady
Claremeore, OK 74017
800-469-5929
FAX: 918-342-2324
<www.p-a-r.org>

Society for Auditory Intervention Techniques (SAIT)
P. O. Box 4538
Salem, OR 97302
<www.teleport.com/~sait/table.html>

- **Attention Deficit Disorder: What Teachers Should Know**
  <www.chadd.org/doe/doe_tc>

- **Auditory Integration Training and the Counseling Center**
  <http://www.vision3d.com/adhd/index.shtml>

- **National Center for Learning Disabilities**
  <www.ncld.org/ld/info_ld2.html>
  <www.ncld.org/brochures/geninfo.html>

■ ■

Notes

■ ■

Management and Intervention Issues

A speech-language pathologist consulted with school-based teachers working with a three-year-old girl who was deaf and blind. The team of teachers included a special education teacher, a speech-language pathologist, a specialist of vision-impaired clients, and an adapted physical education teacher. Every day, the little girl was "pulled out" of her self-contained special education classroom to work with each specialist.

The consultant observed the girl try to cautiously navigate the special ed classroom, running her outstretched hand over a chair before sitting. The consultant was surprised when the teacher asked, "What can I do to help her navigate the hallways so she'll know where the different rooms are located?" "Have you discussed this with the vision-impaired specialist?" the consultant asked. The teacher's response was even more surprising, "I never get a chance to talk with her." Yet the specialist took the little girl from this teacher's room every day.

When the consultant asked the specialists what type of intervention approach they used, each called it a "multidisciplinary team." The consultant was surprised by their answer. Many different disciplines (educators, speech-language pathologists, vision-impaired specialists) provided services to the girl, but a "team approach" obviously did not exist in this case. There was no consensus of goals or strategies, there was no sharing of roles and responsibilities. They didn't even have time to talk to each other! The consultant's first recommendation to the principal of the school was to provide the team with time to meet weekly to talk about the children under their care. Time to team—an essential component to a team approach.

A team approach is undoubtedly the best way to manage LD. An effective management and intervention plan also includes concerns such as assessment results, parental and familial concerns, the strengths and weaknesses of the individual, and a range of special factors like positive behavior management strategies and assistive technology. In this chapter, we will discuss at length, team models, approaches, and strategies. We will also address specific concerns parents might have, and strategies that people with learning disabilities might use as adults—specifically, educational and vocational issues.

A frog once asked two geese to take him South. "How could it be done?" the geese wondered. The frog suggested they hold a stick in their beaks and he would hold on to it with his mouth. So off went the unlikely threesome, flying southward over the countryside. People looked up and admired this demonstration of creative teamwork. Someone exclaimed, "It's wonderful! Who was so clever to discover such a fine way to travel?" Whereupon the frog opened his mouth and said, "It was I," and he plummeted to the earth.

Teams . . . .

Children with learning disabilities have a wide range of debilitating conditions that require special teaching techniques. No one professional has all of the knowledge and skills to identify, assess, and teach every child. It takes a team. A typical team might include regular and special education teachers, academic specialists and related personnel, and parents. The team is responsible for assessing the child and developing and implementing an individualized education program (IEP).

Members

A *team* is a group of one or more people who combine to contribute a clearly defined share of effort in a cooperative, problem-solving process to reach a mutual goal (Dettmer 1996). There are two kinds of team members.

- *Core team members* are most directly involved in designing and implementing and/or monitoring a plan.

- *Support team members* are usually available as needed. They do not have frequent or regularly scheduled interactions with the child or with the core team. They can provide special expertise not available among the core team.

Purpose

The *purpose* of a team is to:

- identify problems, issues, and their potential solutions

- implement solutions to the problems and issues

- monitor the effectiveness of the solutions

- offer solutions until problems and issues are addressed to the satisfaction of the individual with the disability, the family, and other professionals

The Language of Teams

When members talk about an effective team, you'll hear comments like, "Everyone is on the same page. Everyone is comfortable with one another. Everyone has faith in each others' skills. We work well together. We work like a well-oiled machine."

Sometimes you'll find yourselves on teams that don't work. You'll hear language like, "We never seem to see eye-to-eye. She always has to have the last word. He always has to have it his way. He never is prepared." When teams don't work, the core members or team leader must assume a leadership role and enact steps to develop effective teaming or collaborative behaviors.

Team Behaviors

There are two categories of behaviors for effective teams: work-related and affective-interpersonal (Phoenix International 1993). Effective teams tend to have members with characteristics in both categories.

Work-Related Behaviors	Affective-Interpersonal Behaviors
• self-imitates	• listens
• asks questions	• reinforces other members
• provides information	• encourages participation
• possesses good communication skills	• is willing to be flexible
• clarifies information	• strives to reduce/eliminate conflict
• summarizes information	
• demonstrates good problem-solving skills	
• shares leadership/participant roles	
• cooperates to form goals	

Models

It takes time and effort for members to become comfortable with one another and to feel safe with each others' decisions and personal and professional styles. Hence, the word team*work*. Teams generally work within a consultant model or a collaborative model. *Consultants* have specialized knowledge or skills in an area that other team members lack. They are often termed "experts," and they interact with the team as needed. Teams tend to work best when members collaborate. *Collaboration* is "a style for direct interaction between at least two coequal parties voluntarily engaged in shared decision making as they work toward a common goal" (Friend and Cook 1996).

Collaborative relationships improve when people understand themselves and others better. Personality inventories have been widely used to help groups recognize their organizational style and to improve their communication with one another. The Myers Briggs Type

Inventory (MBTI) and the Richardson Inventory of Personality Type (RIPT) provide insight into an individual's personality and can be valuable tools for improving collaborative relationships (Richardson and Stoehr 1998). Understanding if someone is an introvert or extrovert can help avoid a divisive working relationship filled with resentment and distrust.

Federal Mandates

The structure and function of educational teams have evolved because of federal mandates. A little historical context will help you understand this evolution.

P.L. 94-142

The *Education for All Handicapped Children Act of 1975* (P.L. 94-142) contained several features that directly impacted children with special needs and the professionals who served them. Regular and special educators needed to work together to provide all children with disabilities a free and appropriate education (FAPE) within various educational settings (e.g., regular and special education classrooms, resource classrooms).

Special education and related services were provided without cost to the students with exceptionalities or to their parents. Each student who received special education and/or related services had to have an individualized education program (IEP) developed by a multidisciplinary team. The IEP had to be implemented in the least restrictive environment (LRE) appropriate. Parents were granted the right to participate in all aspects of their child's assessment, placement, and education program. Teachers, related professionals, and parents became the core members of the student's educational team.

IDEA

In 1990, the *Education for All Handicapped Children's Act* was retitled and amended by P.L. 101-476, *Individuals with Disabilities Education Act* (IDEA). IDEA extended the services for children with disabilities and emphasized the importance of educating special students with their nondisabled peers to the greatest extent possible. It also stressed the importance of helping students with disabilities transition from school to post-school settings (i.e., school to work, school to consumer). Regular and special educators and related professionals (e.g., speech-language pathologists, physical and occupational therapists, school psychologists) had to work even more closely to support the inclusion of students with disabilities into regular education classes. Support team members expanded to include community-based consultants such as employers, retail stores, and transportation services.

IDEA was reauthorized in 1997 as P.L. 105-17, and the "new IDEA" continues to provide educational services for children with special needs such as behavior problems. It also added a new section to the IEP requirements that included "special factors" as a component. Some special factors include the child's language and communication needs, the need for assistive technology devices and services, and the need for positive behavioral support. Members of the IEP team expanded to include regular educators, related personnel, and parents (IDEA Comparison Chart, 2000; IDEA Summary, 2000).

Team Types . . . .

There are three types of team models: interdisciplinary, multidisciplinary, and transdisciplinary. Each shares a common feature: a team leader plus one or more members. Each type differs in roles, responsibilities, and collaborative features.

Interdisciplinary

Inter- means "between, among, shared by, or occurring between." Each member independently develops and implements a plan. Results and/or recommendations are shared between the team leader and the other team members. Collaboration with the other team members may be haphazard; not all members may be contacted, but contact with the team leader always takes place. The interdisciplinary model is commonly found in medicine.

For example, a condition is uncovered during an examination by the primary physician. The primary physician refers the patient to a specialist (e.g., psychologist) who examines the patient and refers him to a psychometrist for specific tests. The psychometrist consults with the psychologist who makes a diagnoses and gives the patient a plan for treatment. The psychologist contacts the referring primary physician and provides an update on his/her patient's condition.

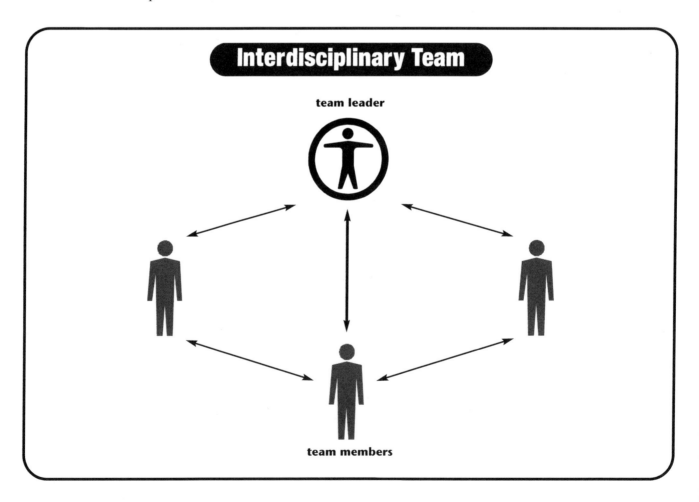

Interdisciplinary Team

team leader

team members

Multidisciplinary

Multi- means "more than two." In a multidisciplinary team, each member independently develops and implements a plan and then shares the results with the team leader. There may be no interaction or collaboration with any other team members.

In reality, nearly all multidisciplinary teams operate like an interdisciplinary team because most teams who identify as multidisciplinary do not operate as independent members. Members collaborate with one another and with the team leader. Because they are composed of professionals from many different disciplines, they have assumed the title but not the function of a multidisciplinary team. When members operate independently and don't collaborate, team members often feel like "the left hand doesn't know what the right hand's doing." Contradictory diagnosis and recommendations can arise, and families are often confused about which information or recommendation they should follow.

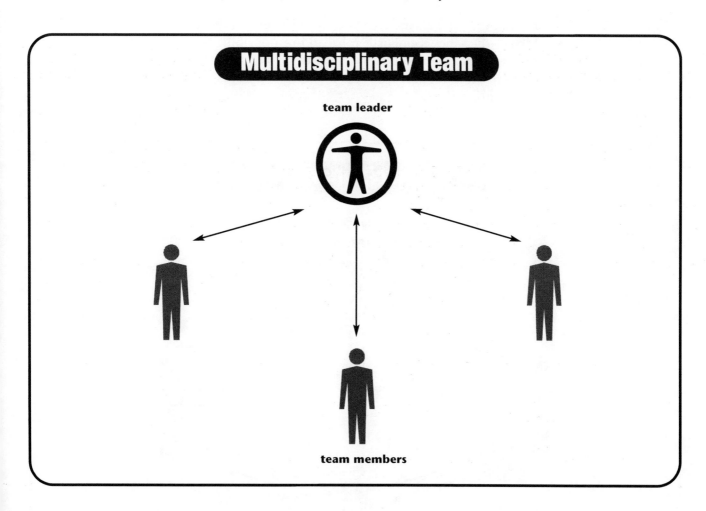

Transdisciplinary

Unlike the first two models, transdisciplinary team members exchange roles and responsibilities across disciplines. Professionals share knowledge and skills, and eventually assume tasks that are traditionally considered *outside* their scope of practice.

For example, a speech-language pathologist and a regular education teacher work together. Usually, the SLP includes activities in her lesson plan that will increase the student's phonological reading skills, and the regular educator facilitates the student's conversational skills during classroom discussions. In this case, the regular education teacher releases some of the responsibility of teaching beginning decoding skills to the speech-language pathologist. In turn, the SLP releases some of the responsibility for enhancing the student's conversational skills to the regular educator because the teacher facilitates the student's conversational skills in the classroom.

The roles of both professionals are enriched because new information from one discipline has been added to the other. Similarly, roles and responsibilities are expanded and exchanged when the professionals infuse activities from each others' disciplines into the student's program. Role support from the professionals is essential to the success of the transdisciplinary process.

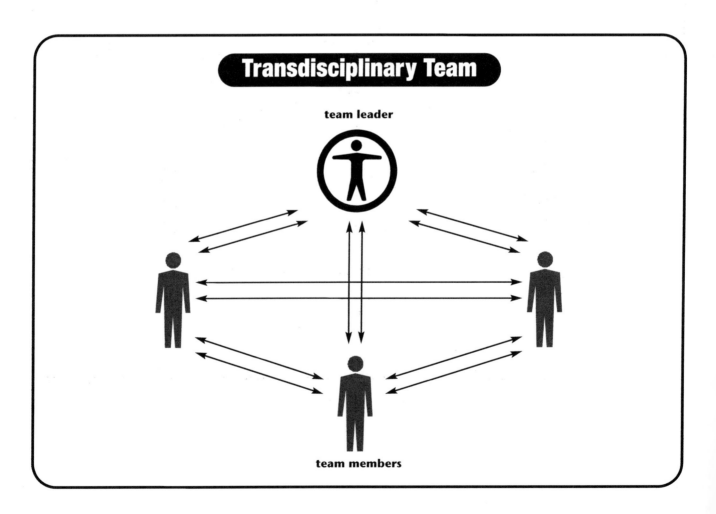

Intervention Models ....

Background

In 1975, Public Law 94-142 mandated that students with disabilities receive free, appropriate education (FAPE) in the least restrictive environment (LRE). Students with disabilities, regardless of the type or severity of the disability, were eligible to receive a public education and related services from 3-21 years of age. A continuum of services for students with disabilities evolved and included regular class, resource rooms, separate or self-contained classes, separate schools, residential facilities, and homebound or hospital settings. The most common placement for students with disabilities was the resource room—a special education classroom where the student received specialized instruction for part of the day.

Regular and special educators, politicians, and parents began to question the efficacy of this dual system of regular education vs. special education. A merger of regular and special education was proposed because special education was costly, and programs for children who were at-risk often overlapped with programs for children with mild disabilities. Many at-risk students were not being served at all. The movement to merge special education with regular education was referred to as the regular education initiative (REI).

IDEA (1990) reflects the philosophy promoted by REI. It mandates that students with disabilities be educated with their nondisabled peers to the greatest extent possible. Educators now have to justify why students with disabilities *cannot* be educated with nondisabled students in the regular classroom. This shift in philosophy to include children with disabilities with regular education students is called *inclusion*.

Inclusion

Inclusion is the goal of integrating students with disabilities into the same classroom, community activities, resources, and home settings as students who do not have disabilities. It means no longer segregating students with disabilities into separate classrooms, schools, transportation, and living arrangements (Turnbull 1999). Inclusion is also described as a "social philosophy that is evidenced in education by the belief and practice that all students are entitled to be important and valued members of their neighborhood school communities" (Friend and Cook 1996).

Inclusion has drastically changed intervention models for students with disabilities. Educators and related personnel such as occupational, speech and physical therapists, psychologists, and reading specialists must now collaborate to design and deliver effective intervention. Three ways of making inclusion possible are through accommodations, adaptations, and modifications.

Accommodations

Accommodations to the curriculum are changes in the way the student receives instruction (e.g., visual vs. auditory, peer tutoring) or produces work (e.g., speaks rather than writes, extended time for test taking). Accommodations support the students' strengths and diminish their weaknesses. "It merely provides the extra time, the special setting, and/or the added assistance that enables accurate assessment of the students' real knowledge rather than assessment of the disability" (Bulletin 1903, 1993).

Modifications

Modifications are the ways educators or related personnel modify, adapt, or change the student's academic material from the work required of other students in the same class ("General Education Access Guide" 1998). A modification does not change the amount of work required, but it may require a change in the instructional level, content, performance criteria, or test format. Modifications increase the student's likelihood for success when he is placed in the least restrictive environment. See the *Suggestion for Adaptations* chart on pages 160 and 161 for further information.

Adaptations

Educators increase the likelihood that students will be successfully included into the academic setting by making adaptations to the curriculum. *Adaptations* are modifications in the instructional and assessment procedures that support the student and accommodate the disability. Adaptations are accommodations and modifications made by educators to the instructional and assessment procedures. Adaptations are identified in the student's educational program.

Multisensory Learning

There are many intervention models and strategies for teaching people with learning disabilities. Some models emphasize an auditory approach, others concentrate on the visual-motor channel, and still others emphasize the auditory-visual connection to learning. Specific strategies reflect a model's emphasis, and the strategies are selected based on the person's strengths and weaknesses. For example, teachers may use a phonics approach to teach reading to children with visual perceptual difficulties. Children with auditory processing deficits may be taught to read by using a visually-oriented, whole-word approach.

Most interventionists, however, support a multisensory approach to teaching people with learning disabilities. Multisensory strategies incorporate the auditory, visual, tactile, and kinesthetic channels for learning. Students listen, look, touch and move as they learn new concepts and practice basic skills. Multisensory activities capitalize on the student's strengths while they diminish the weaknesses.

On pages 160-161, we will look at several Suggestions for Adaptations. The sections are Communication, Reading, Writing, Math, and ADD/ADHD.

Suggestions for Adaptations

Disorder	Accommodation	Modification
Communication	provide model for student to imitate repeat then rephrase instructions use a tape recorder for student to record own speech for self-correction give assignments in small groups to facilitate language development allow student to speak or read aloud first to reduce anxiety	allow advanced practice of oral presentations eliminate competitive practice activities (e.g., timed drills, spelling bees) accept oral responses commensurate with language abilities have student read orally to teacher or peer
Reading	read assignment orally to student use variety of teaching methods and materials allow student to use books on tape or have peers read aloud allow student to read aloud or silently, whichever is the most comfortable and increases comprehension	use word banks and personal dictionaries display and use rule/pronunciation guide reduce amount of text by providing condensed notes of the assignment pair written word with picture of word representing meaning color-code sound and word patterns
Writing	use oral responses to written assignments or tests allow use of word processors, spell checkers, grammar checkers, and word prediction software extend time to complete assignments	judge spelling only on spelling tests accept legible cursive or manuscript handwriting allow student to dictate written assignments to peer recorder approve the use of outlines and visual organizers

Suggestions for Adaptations, *continued*

Disorder	Accommodation	Modification
Math	use manipulatives allow use of calculator allow student to answer orally provide a recorder or have peer write or transfer written work or answers use graph paper to write individual digits in number problems extend time to complete assignments	reduce difficulty of reading level for word problems allow student to use strategies during assignments and tests grade pass/fail or change the grading scale
ADD/ADHD	break tasks into sequential steps reduce or minimize distractions place students near instructor use study carrels in the classroom provide small group or individualized instruction demonstrate task before asking student to perform it	include/increase visual cues in notebooks, workbooks, and assignments use visual organizers to solve problems have student summarize instructions before beginning tasks reduce the number of items on assignments and tests

Intervention Methods . . . .

Students with LD learn in a variety of ways. They have strengths and weaknesses that educators have to recognize to plan education programs accordingly. Foundation skills such as communication and problem solving used for meeting academic requirements and "the world beyond" are embedded in the content standards of subjects; for example, English/language arts, mathematics, science, social studies, foreign language, and arts. Benchmarks for content standards typically identify and describe what students are expected to learn ("General Education Access Guide" 1998). Individualized education programs help educators deliver the required foundation and subject-specific knowledge and skills, and benchmarks are a measure of the student's outcome.

Instruction may be teacher-directed, student-centered, or a combination of the two. **Teacher-directed learning** gives students the skills to read and spell words, to master math facts, and to comprehend oral and written information. Teachers provide direct instruction and guide students through activities where the skills are practiced. Eventually, students practice the skills until they are independent or until the performance criterion is met.

Mastery of the skill, however, is not realized until the student generalizes the skill to new or unique situations. **Student-directed learning** allows some freedom in selecting and implementing academic objectives and activities. Exploratory learning with activities that require application of knowledge and self-evaluation are components of student-directed activities.

Educators have to match the most effective intervention to help the learner acquire and generalize knowledge and skills. Five of the more common collaborative intervention methods found in inclusive settings will be discussed here. Keep in mind that these are only a few of many special intervention methods.

1. Co-Teaching

Co-teaching involves two or more teachers who plan and deliver instruction as co-equals in one educational setting to one group of students (Dettmer 1996). It's often referred to as **team teaching**, whereby a group of educators cooperatively plans and delivers instruction as a unit.

Here are three ways to implement co-teaching: teach and monitor, parallel teaching, and learning centers (Dettmer 1996).

- **Teach and Monitor**. In teach and monitor, one educator is responsible for teaching while the other monitors the students' work. This approach capitalizes on the teachers' strengths and interests. The monitor can provide students who are not succeeding with individualized instruction and learning strategies. The teachers have to diligently review their teaching/monitoring responsibilities and strive for a shared partnership.

- **Parallel teaching.** Parallel teaching involves planning by both teachers, but each one teaches the lesson to a small group of students at the same time—paralleling each other. It allows for a smaller student-to-teacher ratio, which increases participation and attention. It also allows the teachers to work with homogenous groups of students (e.g., more or less advanced) so concepts and pace of the lesson can be adapted to needs. Teachers have to be careful that groups aren't used in such a way that the students in one group become artificially or informally labeled "the special ed kids."

- **Learning centers.** Learning centers have been used for many years in early intervention, regular, and special education classrooms. Learning centers can be set up so that students rotate from one station to another, meeting and working with the teachers, or the teachers may move from center to center working with small groups of students. Students have to be able to work at some level of independence and in small groups for this type of co-teaching to be successful. Centers can present activities that require different levels of knowledge and skills from the students, and the activities can be modified to meet the students' learning styles.

2. Paraeducator/Paraprofessional/Support Personnel

Para means "beside, beyond, helping in a secondary way, accessory." Para-educators, paraprofessionals, and support personnel usually have less formal educational training than the person they work with, but they often have as much or more hands-on training. "Paras" do not function independently of the person for whom they are working. The teacher directs the paraeducator and the speech-language pathologist directs the support personnel such as a speech assistant.

Support personnel, however, can competently implement basic educational and functional goals under the direction and supervision of a mentor. They can implement practice drills and repetitive exercises, and collect data about the students' performances. They cannot evaluate, diagnose, or design individualized education programs. Paraprofessionals are valued members of the team and provide much needed assistance.

3. Peer Tutoring

Peer tutoring is the instruction of one student by another for the purposes of instructional and social support (Turnbull 1996). Educators have paired students for many years. One student can often explain concepts and skills to another student in ways only the other can understand. Peer tutoring frees the teacher to act as a consultant to the peer group. Teachers have to monitor the members' levels of independence to ensure that both members are accountable for their own work.

4. Cooperative Learning Groups

Cooperative or group learning "provides the structure for students to work together toward mutual goals and emphasizes the importance of having all members in the group work together to achieve their individual and collective goals" (Turnbull 1996). Students work in heterogeneous groups and practice/apply previously presented knowledge or skills (Dettmer 1996). Cooperative groups can be used across the curriculum for a variety of content standards and benchmarks. Teachers need to consider grouping students appropriately, managing instructional time, and tracking outcomes. Many use cooperative learning for "hands-on" activities that require applying knowledge learned from discussions or readings. Teachers can modify the activity to meet the needs and objectives of individuals in the group, but the group typically shares a common goal. For example:

Group outcome: to conduct a chemistry experiment and record the observations from the experiment
Individual objectives: Student accurately measures chemicals using a beaker with metric units.
Individual modifications: Student dictates the observations to a peer recorder.

5. Thematic or Topic Instruction

Thematic instruction uses a *theme* or a *topic* to increase knowledge and skills. Themes can be applied across the curriculum to include subject-specific knowledge/skills and foundation skills. A thematic organizer can help educators plan instructional goal activities that will integrate the theme across the curriculum.

In thematic or topic instruction, teachers generally begin by asking students about their personal knowledge of a topic, and what they would like to know about it. Their knowledge is expanded by activities that are often student-centered. They choose a particular method for acquiring and demonstrating knowledge and skills. For example:

Theme: Geography

Prior Personal Knowledge: student has visited a desert and a swamp

Knowledge: Learn and present information about physical differences between two regions (e.g., deserts and swamps).

Skills: • Accessing resources
• Communication (verbal or written)

Sources: • Read encyclopedia (print or electronic).
• Other: student suggests a source for learning

Activities: • Write a resource paper on the topic.
• Create a map-making activity.

Teacher accommodates the student's learning style, strengths, and weaknesses by offering a variety of sources and activities for the student to acquire and demonstrate knowledge about geography. A thematic organizer is on page 165.

Thematic Organizer

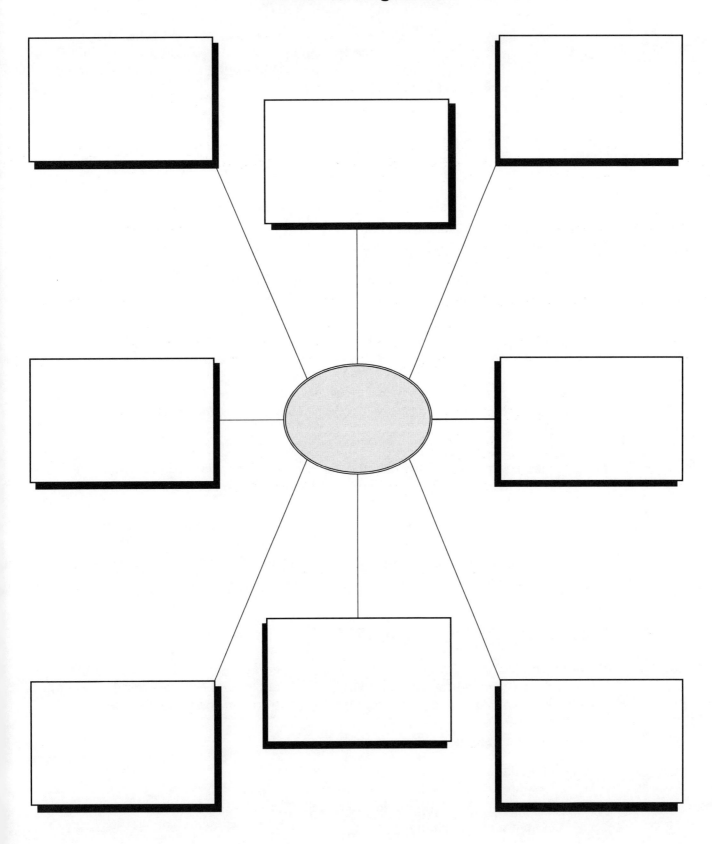

Roles and Responsibilities for Parents . . . .

Parents report feelings of shock, disbelief, depression, shame, and grief when they first hear that their child has a disability. Teachers and personnel in related disciplines need to help parents deal with these feelings. Until parents understand and cope with their own feelings, they can't adequately help their child.

How Parents Can Cope

Here are some tips to help parents accept their child's disability:

- Relay the diagnosis with empathy and realistic expectations. Try not to speculate what a young child will or will not be capable of doing as an adult.

- Provide information and resources about the disability. Schools may provide parent-to-parent support groups that are moderated by a school psychologist, social worker, or counselor. The adage, "They will hear when they are ready to hear" certainly applies when counseling parents of children with disabilities.

- Encourage parents to ask questions. Restate the parents' statements or perceptions to ensure accuracy of information and to reduce misperceptions.

- Seek and provide answers to the parents' questions when you can, but admit to not knowing some of the answers when you don't have them.

- Parents progress through stages of adjustment similar to those associated with death that include shock, denial, anger, depression, and acceptance. Recognize the stages of adjustment and support parents through the passage of emotions.

Roles, Responsibilities, and the IDEA

Parents of children with learning disabilities are recognized as critical members in the evaluation and intervention process. The Individuals with Disabilities Education Act (IDEA) refined and expanded parental roles and responsibilities to include the following tips.

When evaluating a student:

- obtain informed consent from the parents before the evaluation is conducted

- include information from the parents that can help the team determine the existence of a disability

When reevaluating a student:

- inform the parents that additional information is needed for a reevaluation and give the reasons for it

- inform the parents that they have the right to request an assessment to determine if their child continues to have a disability

IFSP and IEP

When developing an Individual Family Service Plan (IFSP) or an Individual Education Program (IEP):

- The local educational agency must ensure that the parents are part of any group that makes decisions about their child's educational placement.

- Parents of preschool children with a disability may have an IFSP instead of an IEP.

- Parents who transition from early intervention services to preschool services will meet at least 90 days before the child is eligible for services. The child may receive preschool and other appropriate services at age three.

- A statement identifying how the parents will be regularly informed about their child's progress must be included. Parents of children with disabilities will be informed of their child's progress at least as often as parents of nondisabled children.

When parents disagree with a placement:

- They can request a hearing. The state education agency or local education agency must arrange for a hearing. The child remains in an interim, alternative educational setting (IAES) pending the hearing officer's decision. The child may be placed in the IAES for up to 45 days.

- The cost of education of a child with a disability in a private school may be reduced:

    ✔ if the parents did not inform the IEP team that they were rejecting the recommended placement of the public agency, or if the parents fail to give the public agency written notice within ten business days before removing their child from the public agency's educational setting

✔ if, before the parents remove their child from the public agency's educational setting, the public agency informs the parents of its intent to evaluate the child, but the parents fail to make the child available for the evaluation, or a court rules the parents' actions are unreasonable

✔ if the agency did not make a free appropriate public education (FAPE) available to the child in a timely manner prior to enrollment in the private school (Primer on IDEA 1997 and Its Regulations 1999)

Parents as Advocates

The following tips can help parents be advocates for their children ("How Parents Can Be Advocates" 2000):

1. **Know the rules**.
   All public schools follow minimum federal standards that provide special services for children with disabilities. Contact your local school district office or state Department of Education for specific laws and regulations and obtain your state's criteria for eligibility.

2. **Get to know the people who make decisions about your child's education.**
   Talk with your child's teachers, principal, and support personnel on a regular basis. If your concerns or problems aren't adequately addressed, follow the procedures for your school/school district.

3. **Keep records.**
   Maintain a file of educational records including evaluations and IEPs. Take notes during telephone and personal conferences. Keep examples of your child's work to document abilities and progress.

4. **Gather information**.
   Increase your awareness about the issues. Research and read information about laws, learning disabilities, assessment and intervention techniques, etc.

5. **Join with others who care**.
   Join support groups and professional organizations in your area and state. Become familiar with educational jargon. Ask questions and don't be embarrassed to ask for clarification or examples if the information is unclear.

6. **Communicate effectively**.
   Go to meetings prepared. Have materials and questions prepared ahead of time. Listen, speak clearly, and put things in writing whenever possible.

7. **Know your child's strengths and interests and share them with educators.**
Your child's strengths and interests provide insight into the whole child and could assist educators in identifying learning styles and accommodations.

8. **Emphasize solutions.**
Stress the positive and help educators identify ways to improve your child's experiences. Monitor your child's work daily and follow through with agreed-on strategies.

9. **Focus on the big picture.**
Look at the whole educational experience and the process for obtaining the most appropriate education. Try not to let arguments over details impede the rapport and communication you have with your child's teachers.

10. **Involve your child in decision making.**
Learning disabilities are life-long issues and self-advocacy is one of the keys to becoming a successful adult. Talk with your child about his disability, encourage him to learn more about it, and include him in IEP meetings.

Higher Education & The World of Work . . . .

Successful transition from high school to post-secondary school (college or university) or to the work world require informed choices. The following tips will help you make a smoother transition.

Transition from High School

Learning disabilities do *not* disappear when a student graduates from high school—they persist into adulthood. Disabilities can consist of a variety of disorders, including difficulties in listening, speaking, reading, writing, social skills, and math. Many adults are identified as having a learning disability after they drop out of or graduate from high school. If you would like to screen yourself or another adult for learning disabilities, see the Adult Dyslexia Checkist in the references (Lee 2000).

The Rehabilitation Act of 1973 and the American with Disabilities Act of 1990 (ADA) prohibit discrimination against children and adults with disabilities. The Rehabilitation Act applies to public and private elementary and secondary schools and colleges that receive federal funding. It also applies to employers that receive federal funding. The ADA applies to all public and most private schools and colleges regardless of federal funding, to private employers with fifteen or more employees, and to state and local governments (Latham 1996).

Adults with learning disabilities may encounter these difficulties:

- completing applications for college enrollment or employment due to poor reading and writing skills

- meeting timelines for class or job requirements because of poor planning, inadequate organizational skills, and inattention to details

- interacting socially with peers or employers because of misinterpreting others' moods and attitudes

- dealing with low self-esteem, which reduces the person's independence or ability to be a self advocate

- being responsible for daily living activities such as banking and check writing, taking phone messages, filing tax returns, etc.

Finding the Right College

Many high school graduates with learning disabilities complete undergraduate and graduate education if they are provided appropriate accommodations. College accommodations depend on the disability and how it impacts the student's learning. High school students should contact their counselor or the university's registrar to get information on special arrangements for taking the SAT and/or ACT. Examination options might include taking untimed tests, having the test read to the student, or listening to the test on cassette.

Every student wants to find the right college or university. A student with a learning disability might require extra time and information to find the best match. Here are some questions to help students with their college search (Block 2000).

1. Is there a separate admission criteria, process, and fee for students with learning disabilities?

2. What documentation is required to validate the diagnosis of learning disability?

3. How are accommodations determined? Who determines them?

4. Are remedial or developmental courses offered? Are they credited toward graduation?

5. What devices and support services are offered? Are there fee devices or services such as:

   - tape recorders
   - alternative forms of testing
   - note takers

- typing services
- tutors
- counseling

6. Is career planning offered?

7. Does the administration and faculty support programs and students with learning disabilities?

Tips for College Students and Instructors

College and university support service personnel, students, and instructors should work together to develop appropriate accommodations for students' learning disabilities. A profile of learning styles (Lee 1999) and the following tips for college-bound high school students with LD (Mahoney-Kuba 2000) provide students, instructors, and university support personnel with useful strategies and information.

- Remind students that they can take a college class prior to full-time registration to understand expectations, build their confidence, and determine what kind of accommodations they may need.

- Make sure learning is structured and multisensory.

- Help students and their advisors determine the best majors and types of classes (e.g., distance learning, lecture, lab).

- Provide a lot of exposure to new and abstract concepts. Students with LD have difficulty grasping abstract concepts especially when they are presented in new and decontextualized ways. Attention and memory deficits can also reduce comprehension.

- Encourage students to find study groups they can meet with regularly to review notes and discuss assignments and lecture information.

- Relate abstract concepts to previously learned concepts.

- Have students verbalize information in their own words to check comprehension.

- Ask students for examples to help with generalization.

- Recognize that strengths and weaknesses may be specific to certain skills. Some students will excel in verbal assignments and perform poorly on written tasks.

- Provide options when giving assignments (e.g., portfolio vs. research paper, designing and building a model vs. an oral presentation describing a model).

- Allow students to use technology (e.g., laptop computers with spelling and grammar checkers for in-class note taking and assignments, tape recorders).

- Teach paced learning.

- Monitor the amount and pace with which information is disseminated. Reduce the amount of information and assess comprehension with regular assessments.

- Reduce anxiety by increasing time limits.

- Extend time for in-class and test-taking activities. Reading and writing difficulties increase the amount of time it takes someone with LD to complete an assignment.

Transitions to Work

Adults with learning disabilities may describe themselves as capable in many areas, and at the same time, experience difficulties meeting deadlines or keeping appointments, reading technical reports, writing memos, or expressing themselves verbally in meetings. These difficulties may cause frustration, embarrassment, or anxiety. These adults may try to conceal the difficulties from their employers or co-workers, they may withdraw from opportunities for advancement for fear their difficulties may surface, or they can delay completing assignments.

Weaknesses in reading and writing, memory, sequencing, visual orientation, hand-eye coordination, expressive language, organizational skills, and interpersonal relationships affect efficiency at work in a number of ways (Moody 1999).

Adults with LD may have difficulty:

Reading and Writing
- following written directions
- reading or writing reports quickly and efficiently
- writing memos and letters

Memory
- remembering telephone numbers, messages, and instructions
- taking notes or recalling information presented at meetings

Sequencing
- alphabetizing files
- using alphabetically organized reference materials
- writing strings of numbers or spelling words correctly

Visual Orientation
- locating meeting rooms or materials in a warehouse
- reading blueprints, maps, tables, and charts
- traveling by car to unfamiliar cities or finding the correct terminal/ baggage claims area in airports

Hand-Eye Coordination
- handwriting notes or correspondence quickly and neatly
- encoding data using a calculator, key pad, or word processor
- keyboarding quickly
- transferring information from a ledger to computer, from invoice to ledger, etc.

Expressive Language
- with word-retrieval or word-finding
- organizing oral presentations
- avoiding extensive fillers or stallers such as "um," "like," etc.
- speaking without relying on gestures to communicate

Organizational Skills
- making notes or to-do lists, losing or forgetting to refer to them
- keeping deadlines (gets the day, time, or place for meetings wrong)
- keeping materials for meetings

Interpersonal Relationships
- being assertive to hide from disability
- controlling defensiveness due to heightened sensitivity about disability

Workplace Accommodations

Workplace accommodations are developed on an individual basis between employee and employer. The number and type of accommodations depend on how the disabilities impact job performance. Solutions may involve work-site modifications, flexibility in work schedules, equipment adaptations, or a job-training specialist to support the person with a learning disability during training. Here are some tips for adults who want to succeed in the workplace.

- Complete a vocational assessment to identify aptitudes, strengths, and weaknesses.

- Seek out part-time jobs or volunteer to improve interpersonal skills to better understand work situations and expectations.

- Know your learning style and match it with different vocations and jobs.

- Apply for jobs for which you have the knowledge, skills, and abilities.

- Conduct on-site visits to better understand different work environments and jobs.

- Request job descriptions before applying for a position.

- Know how and when to request appropriate accommodations.

- Describe strategies and accommodations that assist in job performance.

- Establish benchmarks and evaluation timelines so you and your employer can review your performance and the effectiveness of any accommodations (Payne 1995; "Preparing" 2000).

Summary . . . .

Teamwork is the best way to serve people with LD. Management and intervention models are effective when those responsible for their implementation understand themselves and others. Professionals who work together to serve students with learning disabilities have to recognize differences between and among the people in the group. These differences do not have to be barriers to effective teaming, but when they prevent the group from working collaboratively, changes must be made.

Teams work in different ways, but regardless of the model under which they work, their goal is to provide appropriate services for the individual. Intervention strategies are driven by the needs of each student. Educators have to understand their responsibility to make adaptations in their teaching styles and to the student's curriculum in order to provide the most appropriate education. Selecting and implementing intervention strategies that best match the student's needs with the academic standards are the responsibility of the team. Parents are also key members of the team.

. . . .

References and Resources . . . .

Block Educational Consulting, "Questions to Ask During the College Search," *Newsletter for Guidance Counselors, Students with Learning Disabilities, Parents and Teachers*, 2000.

"Bulletin 1903: Regulations for the Implementation of R.S. 17:7(11)," The Louisiana Dyslexia Law, Louisiana Department of Education, Baton Rouge, LA, 1993.

Cramer, S. F., *Collaboration: A Success Strategy for Special Educators*, Allyn & Bacon, Boston, 1998.

Dettmer, P. A., Dyck, N. T., and Thurston, L. P., *Consultation, Collaboration, and Teamwork for Students with Special Needs*, Allyn & Bacon, Boston, 1996.

Friend, M. and Cook, L., *Interactions: Collaboration Skills for School Professionals, 2nd Ed.*, Longman, White Plains, NY, 1996.

"General Education Access Guide: A Tool Kit for Program Development: Draft," Louisiana Department of Education Office of Student & School Performance Division of Special Populations, Baton Rouge, LA, 1998.

Heward, W.L., *Exceptional Children: An Introduction to Special Education, 5th Ed.*, Prentice Hall, Englewood Cliffs, NJ, 1996.

Healey, B., "Helping Parents Deal with the Fact That Their Child Has a Disability," *The Council for Exceptional Children*, 3(5), <http://www.ldonline.org/ld_indepth...ng_techniques/helping_parents.html> (May 2, 2000).

"How Parents Can be Advocates for Their Children," *Coordinated Campaign for Learning Disabilities*, <http:///www.ldonline.org/ld_indepth/parenting/ccld_advocacy.html> (May 2, 2000).

"IDEA Comparison Chart," <http://www.house.gov/ed_workforce/hottopics/idea/idea-sumchart.html> (February 23, 2000).

"IDEA Summary," <http://www.asha.org/idea/idea_summary.html> (February, 23, 2000).

Latham, P.H., "Learning Disabilities and the Law, After High School: An Overview for Students," 1996, <http://www.ldonline.org/ld_indepth/ legal_legislative/latham_ld.html> (May 2, 2000).

Lee, J., "The Learning Styles of Adults with Dyslexia," Dyslexia 2000 Network, <http://www.futurenet.co.uk/charity/ado/adomenu/learnstyl.html> (June 26, 2000).

Louisiana Educational Rights of Exceptional Children Reaching for Results, Louisiana Department of Education, Baton Rouge, LA, July 1999.

Mahoney-Kuba, S., "Tips for College Bound High School Students with Diagnosed Learning Problems," *The Learning Center, Buckhannon*, WV, 2000, <http://www.ldonline.org/ld_indepth/transition/college_tips.html> (May 2, 2000).

Moody, S., "Dyslexia in the Workplace," *Dyslexia 2000 Network*, <http://www.futurenet. co.uk/charity/ado/index.html> (May 13, 2000).

Payne, N., "Tips for Workplace Success for the Adult Learner," Linkages 2(1), National Adult Literacy and Learning Disabilities Center, 1995, <http://www.ldonline.org/ ld_indepth/adult/payne_workplacetips.html> (May 16, 2000).

"Phoenix International: Checklist for Team Behaviors," 1993.

"Preparing for Postsecondary Education with a Learning Disability: From High School to Higher Education," *A Guide for Students to Make Informed Decisions*, <http://www.latan.org> (June 12, 2000).

"Primer on IDEA 1997 and its Regulations," *Newsletter of the Council for Exceptional Children*, 5(7), April/May, 1999, <http://www.ldonline.org/ld_indepth...al_education/ cec_idea-primer.html> (March 21, 2000).

Richardson, R. and Stoehr, R., "Collaboration Model Collaboration: Building Relationships of Trust & Respect," paper presented at annual meeting of the American Speech-Language-Hearing Association, Seattle, WA, 1998.

Ripich, D. N. and Creaghead, N. A., *School Discourse Problems, 2nd ed.*, Singular, San Diego, 1994.

Turnbull, A., Turnbull, R., Shank, M. and Leal, D., *Exceptional Lives: Special Education in Today's Schools, 2nd Ed.*, Merrill, Upper Saddle River, NJ, 1999.

■ ■

College Resources and School Testing Issues
<http://www.ncld.org/resources/resources3.html>

Employment and Related Issues
<http://www.ncld.org/resources/resources4.html>

Self-Help Organizations
<http://www.asha.org/consumers/selfhelp.html>

■ ■

Notes

■ ■

The glossary lists unfamiliar or important words in the book. Some words may appear in more than one chapter. The chapter(s) where the word(s) appears most prominently is listed at the end of the definition. For example, (1) means that you can find the word in Chapter 1.

accommodations changes in the ways students receive instruction (e.g., visual vs. auditory, multisensory) or the way students produce work (e.g., speaks rather than writes, extended time for test taking); support students' strengths while diminishing weaknesses (8)

adaptations accommodations and modifications made by educators to instructional and assessment practices (8)

affective domain area of human development that deals with emotions, attitudes, values, and interests (2)

algorithm explicit, step-by-step method of computation (6)

articulation disorder atypical production of speech sounds characterized by substitutions, omissions, additions, or distortions that interfere with intelligibility (3)

attention deficit *Type 1*—hyperactivity disorder, combined type: most common subtype; one demonstrates six (or more) symptoms of inattention and six (or more) symptoms of hyperactivity-impulsivity for at least six months
Type 2—hyperactivity disorder, predominantly inattention type: one demonstrates six (or more) symptoms of inattention (but fewer than six symptoms of hyperactivity-impulsivity) for at least six months
Type 3—hyperactivity disorder, predominantly hyperactive-impulsive type: inattention is significant, but six (or more) characteristics of hyperactivity-impulsivity exist for at least six months (7)

cardinal number whole number that expresses how many items are in a set (one, two, three, etc.) (6)

central auditory processing disorder (CAPD) limitation in the expression, analysis, organization, transformation, elaboration, memory, retrieval, and use of information contained in audible signals; not associated with a hearing loss (3) (4)

classification	ability to perceive categorical relationships (6)
cluttering	involves excessive breaks in the normal flow of speech that seem to result from disorganized speech planning, talking too fast or in spurts, or simply being unsure of what one wants to say (3)
collaboration	style for direct interaction between at least two coequal parties voluntarily engaged in shared decision making as they work toward a common goal (8)
communication disorder	impairment in the ability to receive, send, process, and comprehend concepts or verbal, nonverbal and graphic symbol systems; might be evident in hearing, language, and/or speech processes; range in severity from mild to profound; can be developmental or acquired. Persons may demonstrate one or any combination of communication disorders; may result in primary or secondary disability (3)
conductive hearing loss	results from an abnormality in the outer or middle ear. The volume of sounds is reduced and one may have difficulty perceiving speech sounds correctly; can be the result of a temporary condition (e.g., fluid behind the eardrum); generally treated with medications; might be permanent due to a congenital or acquired condition (e.g., scaring of the eardrum) (3)
conservation	substance, length, continuous quantity, number, area, weight, and volume does not change even if an object's appearance changes (6)
cooperative learning group	provides the structure for students to work together toward mutual goals and emphasize importance of having all members in the group work together to achieve their individual and collective goals (8)
core team members	those most directly involved in designing, implementing, and/or monitoring a plan for the person with disabilities (8)
co-teaching	two or more teachers who plan and deliver instruction as co-equals in one educational setting to one group of students (8)
deafness	hearing disorder that limits an individual's aural/oral communication performance to the extent that the primary sensory input for communication may be other than the auditory channel (3)
deductive reasoning	process of reasoning logically from whole-to-part or general-to-specific (6)

dialectical variations	variations in the speech and language systems of people from the same region, social, or cultural and ethnic backgrounds; not considered a communication disorder but a communication variation or difference (3)
dyscalculia	neurologically-based disorder that affects ability to do mathematics (6)
dysgraphia	language processing disorder that affects writing, spelling, written composition, handwriting; sometimes refers to extreme handwriting difficulties only (5)
dyslexia	neurologically-based language processing disorder affecting expressive and/or receptive language (4)
dysnomia	neurologically-based difficulty affecting word retrieval (4)
figure-ground relationships	ability to focus on an object without interference from its setting or background (6)
fluency disorder	interruption in speaking flow characterized by atypical rate, rhythm, and repetitions in sounds, syllables, words, and phrases; can be accompanied by excessive tension, struggle behavior, and secondary mannerisms (3)
graphophonemics	phoneme-grapheme or sound-symbol relationships (e.g., the letter *a* makes the short *a* sound in *cat*) (4)
hard of hearing	hearing disorder (fluctuating or permanent) that adversely affects ability to communicate; one who is hard of hearing relies on the auditory channel as the primary sensory input for communication (3)
hearing disorder	result of impaired auditory sensitivity of the auditory system; might limit the development, comprehension, production, and/or maintenance of speech and/or language; classified according to difficulties in detection, recognition, discrimination, comprehension, and perception of auditory information; the three types of hearing losses are conductive, sensori-motor, and mixed (3)
heuristic	step-by-step strategies to guide students to resolve mathematical tasks (6)
inclusion	the goal of integrating students with disabilities into the same classroom, community activities and resources, and home settings as students who do not have disabilities; means no longer segregating students with disabilities into separate classrooms, schools, transportation, and living arrangements (8)
inductive reasoning	process of reasoning logically from part-to-whole or specific-to-general (6)

interdisciplinary team	each member independently develops and implements a plan; results and/or recommendations are shared between or among the team leader and other team members; collaboration with the other team members may be inconsistent (8)
intervention	a plan that includes all efforts on behalf of a person with disabilities (8)
joint-action routine	occurs between two persons and typically revolves around a familiar, predictable activity (3)
language disorder	impaired comprehension and/or use of spoken, written and/or other symbol systems; may involve, form of language (phonology, morphology, syntax), content of language (semantics), and/or function of language in communication (pragmatics) in any combination (3)
learned helplessness	dependence on others and perception of lack of control of one's life (2)
learning centers	can be set up so students rotate from one station to another meeting and working with the teachers, or the teachers may move from center-to-center working with small groups of students (8)
learning disabilities[1]	The National Institute of Mental Health (NIMH) states that LD affects the ability to either interpret what one sees and hears or to link information from different parts of the brain. The limitations can appear, in many ways, as specific difficulties with spoken and written language, coordination, self-control, or attention. These difficulties extend to school work and can impede learning to read, write, or do math. (1)
learning disabilities[2]	The National Joint Committee on Learning Disabilities (NJCLD) defines LD as heterogeneous group of disorders manifested by significant difficulties in the acquisition and use of listening, speaking, reading, writing, reasoning, or mathematical abilities. The disorders are intrinsic to the individual, presumed to be due to central nervous system dysfunction, and may occur across the life span. (1)
learning disorders[3]	The National Center for Learning Disabilities (NCLD) says LD is diagnosed when achievement on individually administered, standardized tests in reading, math, or written expression is substantially below that expected for age, schooling, and level of intelligence. Learning problems significantly interfere with academic achievement or activities of daily living that require reading, mathematical, or writing skills. (1)
learning disorders[4]	IDEA says LD is a disability involving one or more of the basic psychological processes involved in understanding or in using spoken or written language, which may manifest itself in an imperfect ability to listen, think, speak, read, write, spell, or to do mathematical calculations. (1)

math anxiety	intense fear and avoidance of mathematics (6)
math manipulatives	concrete objects moved about to illustrate mathematical ideas (6)
memory	short term memory—can store data for short duration, limited to about seven chunks at a time; long term—can store data for long duration, nearly unlimited in capacity; active working—can store data while working on it, like temporary storage (6)
mixed hearing loss	combination of conductive and sensori-neural loss; difficulty hearing and understanding sounds (3)
modifications	ways educators or related personnel adapt, modify, or change a student's academic material from the work required of other students in the same class (8)
morphology	system that governs structure of words and construction of word forms; study of the smallest units of meaning in English (3) (4)
multidisciplinary team	members develop and implement plans independently, then share the results with the team leader; there might not be interaction or collaboration with any other team member (8)
multisensory instruction	integrates visual, auditory, tactile, and kinesthetic approaches (4) (5) (6)
number sense	intuition about number relationships that develops gradually from active participation with concrete objects in mathematical situations (6)
one-to-one correspondence	occurs between two sets when one member of either set is paired exactly with one member of the other set (6)
ordering	ability to organize in a logical sequence (6)
ordinal number	whole number in ordered sequence of whole numbers (first, second, third, etc.) (6)
orthography	the way words of a language are represented in print (5)
parallel teaching	involves planning by both teachers, but each one teaches the lesson to a small group of students at the same time (8)
peer tutoring	instruction of one student by another for the purposes of instructional and social support (8)
phonological awareness	cognizance of the phonological (sound) structure of words including the ability to segment and manipulate sounds within words (4)

phonology	sound system of a language and the rules that govern the sound combinations; study of sounds and how they work in the environment (3)
pragmatics	system that combines form and content of language in functional and socially appropriate communication (3)
resilience	the ability to adjust and overcome problems (2)
scaffolding	providing instruction and guidance as needed; withdrawing support as learners no longer need it (6)
semantics	system that governs meanings of words and sentences (3) (4)
sensori-neural hearing loss	results from an abnormality involving inner ear or sensory pathways that lead to the brain; difficulty understanding sounds regardless of the sounds' volume; losses are permanent, and depending on the severity of the loss, the person may benefit from a hearing aid (3)
spatial sense	intuitive feel for one's environment and the objects in it (6)
speech disorder	impairment of the articulation of speech sounds, fluency and/or voice; three kinds: articulation, fluency, and voice disorders (3)
stuttering	abnormal rate and rhythm of speech characterized by repetitions of sounds and syllables, blocking, and prolongations of sounds; excessive tension and struggle behavior may be apparent (3)
support team members/ consultants	persons available as-needed; do not have frequent or regularly scheduled interactions with client with LD or with core team; provide special expertise not available among the core team (8)
syntax	system governing order and combination of words to form sentences, and the relationships among the elements within a sentence (3) (4)
teach and monitor	a classroom with one educator responsible for teaching while another teacher monitors students' work
team	unified group of people who contribute a clearly-defined portion of the effort in a cooperative problem-solving process to reach a shared goal (8)
transdisciplinary team	members exchange roles and responsibilities across disciplines, and often assume responsibilities of other professions (8)
voice disorder	characterized by abnormal production and/or absences of vocal quality, pitch, loudness, resonance, and/or duration inappropriate for a person's age, sex (3)

1-01-987654